CHESAPEAKE
OUTDOOR TALES

CHESAPEAKE
OUTDOOR TALES

Hunting and Fishing by the Tides

C.L. MARSHALL

THE
History
PRESS

Published by The History Press
Charleston, SC
www.historypress.com

First published 2019

Manufactured in the United States

ISBN 9781467144483

Library of Congress Control Number: 2019945071

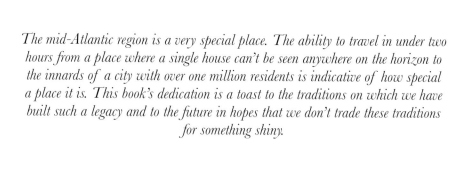

The mid-Atlantic region is a very special place. The ability to travel in under two hours from a place where a single house can't be seen anywhere on the horizon to the innards of a city with over one million residents is indicative of how special a place it is. This book's dedication is a toast to the traditions on which we have built such a legacy and to the future in hopes that we don't trade these traditions for something shiny.

CONTENTS

Courtesy Joyce Northam.

PREFACE

There are things that happen in the field and on the water that defy accurate description via mere words. Sometimes these events are shared with a good friend, but often the ones that stick with us the longest are the ones that we experience alone. There's something therapeutic about taking to the woods or water alone or with the sole companionship of a good dog. The times in which we live have dictated many changes and interruptions in this precious time we spend wandering the marshes and waters of the Chesapeake. The need for a constant stream of information has replaced the ability to read a stream as it makes its way to the headwaters of the Bay. Change is constant. Change is all around us. We must adapt to these changes or be threatened with being left behind.

Sitting on the west side of Spring Island under a June full moon can do wonders for the soul. The peaceful and remote feeling is one that sticks with you. Having a line get tight from time to time doesn't hurt either. Words can't adequately describe this feeling. It must be experienced. It must be lived.

While there's time, take the time to explore the wonders that lie right on our doorstep. Share a blind with a friend. Share a sausage sandwich with a muddy Labrador. Take time to take it in. It's worth it. Tomorrow is promised to no man.

SIXTY DAYS

Sixty days encompass the entirety of waterfowl season in the mid-Atlantic. These precious few days are divided across four months in an effort to provide access to all available species to as many hunters across the region. The various allowable hunting days, or "splits" as they've come to be known, are scrutinized by interested parties from the public comment period through their final publication. Hunters from all parts comment and lobby those wielding the power in hopes of tipping the seasonality of the sport a bit in their favor. In most cases, it's Mother Nature that has the final say on the outcome of the hunter's annual bag.

These allowable hunting days, however, do not make up a hunting season for most avid duck hunters. The season begins long before the first day of the first split dawns. In actuality, it really never ends. But these sixty days represent much more than the opportunity to legally take to the field. It is within these sixty days that much more occurs than the bagging of a few birds. *Tradition, teaching, legacy, heritage, family* and *friendship* are all words that get tossed around in hunting magazines. For those who live them, they are much more than that. For those who live the hunting life, it is part of who they are.

The anticipation of these sixty sunrises and sunsets grows daily, reaching fever pitch on duck season eve. Final preparations for the opener are often made days in advance, but they are checked and rechecked to make certain that all things are in working order. Gunning bags are packed with staples that will be called on throughout the season. Knives are sharpened, calls are

When you're shooting well, a good gun dog can make diver hunting much more enjoyable. *Paul Bramble photo*.

cleaned and tuned, more shells are added to the bag and fresh dog treats are ziplocked tightly.

But waterfowl hunting, more than any other type of hunting, has the capacity to make impressions that last a lifetime. There's a lot of reasons for that. It's a highly social event where idle time is passed in proximity with fellow hunters. It's an environment where much can be shared, and conversation topics contain sporadic serious topics that would not be covered in any other setting. It's permissible to chat about any and all topics. Politics, religion, women, nightlife and even duck hunting are often covered over the course of a hunt. Often long periods of silence are interrupted by random thoughts, observations or possibly even a duck. It's during these periods empty of conversation that much can be learned about ourselves and our partners. There's a lot to soak in during the course of a good duck hunt; words many times obscure an otherwise perfect moment.

To the outsider, duck hunting must seem to be a very, very strange idea. Hunters ritually rise long before the sun, driving a boat through the marshes in total darkness, setting decoys, building hideouts along the reedy shorelines, utilizing a musical instrument to mimic the sounds of ducks and shooting at the ones who mistake this manufactured scenario as they try to escape their mistake. Strange it is indeed, but hunters have been perfecting the craft since time immemorial. For hundreds of years, this activity provided food for the masses, but over time, it became much more than that. Over these years and through direct generational teaching, skills and traditions were passed down, making waterfowl hunting what it is today. Calls, guns and knives are cherished items from hunting partners that hold a special place in the hearts of hunters with whom their protection is entrusted. These things are special for many reasons.

One of the most important and anticipated days of any hunting season is youth day. Most states allot a day solely dedicated to youngsters. Many kids of duck hunters have been tagging along with their parents and their friends for several years. Most surely have willingly accepted invitations to act as labor during the blind building or land prep, awaiting the time when they were ready to shoulder a shotgun. I've witnessed, on many occasions, the most hardcore hunters go all out for youth day long after their kids have surpassed the maximum age limit. There is no satisfaction equaling the sheer excitement in a young hunter's eyes as they enter the brotherhood by loading their guns for the first time. Few things equal the joy as they rise and claim their first duck. Traditions are preserved and initiated at moments such as this.

Within these few precious days of hunting season, many first and lasts often occur. Late winter, spring and summer months are partly taken up by dog training. New pups, with all their curiosity and natural ability, are nonetheless still green. Seeing them progressing to becoming a partner in the hunt from what once was just a small ball of fur a few months ago brings great satisfaction. Good gun dogs don't just happen—they require nurturing with equal doses of discipline. A pup's first retrieve is a momentous thing.

The magic of a marsh coming alive is something that hunters and fishermen alike are privileged to witness. *Coastal Killer photo.*

Folks from the Chesapeake region still take full advantage of living life by the tides. Here a Saxis resident roams the shallows picking soft crabs from the bottom with a long-handled crab net. *C.L. Marshall photo.*

An old partner's last trip is as well. Years of partnership, trust, memories and undeniable loyalty will in time come to an end. When to end a dog's hunting career is not an exact science. A dog's heart and will often overshadow its diminishing physical ability. Relish each trip afield with friends and dogs. There's no telling when either may not be able to answer the call.

The things that make these sixty days memorable are as different as the hunters who take to the field. It is hopes and aspirations. It is the memories that we take back home with us. It's the successes and the failures. It's about you and your two best friends taking five geese in four shots on a bluebird day from a blind that was once shared by your great-grandfather and his friends. It's about the high fives and celebrations that follow. Memories of good dog work, hot soup and grilled sandwiches fill the pages of our minds. Such things often sporadically dance around in our minds during the days ahead and behind those sixty days. But we're an insatiable bunch. The experience is addictive. It's the combination of memories already in the bank and those that lie in front of us that ensures we wake before the alarm on opening day.

Sixty days is all we get. Use them wisely.

FIFTY BLUEBILLS

One couldn't ask for a day more suited for gunning than this December morning. Overcast, temperatures in the upper twenties, occasionally spitting snow and a wind from the northwest gusting at times to twenty-five miles per hour. This weather pattern had held for nearly ten days, pushing large amounts of waterfowl of all species down in the Pocomoke Sound. My father and I were taking full advantage of our good fortune.

The prior afternoon, we had ventured up in the heart of the Saxis Wildlife Management Area, where we were treated to an hour of nonstop shooting. Green-wing teal barreled from the north following a small gut to our decoys. Single and paired black ducks refused to circle the decoys, instead opting for a direct route to our handmade blocks. Five Baldpates fell from the heavens and nervously danced like marionettes above our decoys. The highlight of the afternoon was the half-dozen pintails that rode the strong north winds on cupped wings for what seemed like an eternity before finally committing to the decoys. Through all this action, we watched as flock after flock of bluebills moved from the big waters of the Chesapeake toward the shelter of smaller creeks for the night. Plans were set for the next morning.

When our bag was filled with a fantastic assortment of puddle ducks, we picked up our dozen blocks and idled out of the marsh for a short ride home. Normally, the wind will tend to diminish in the hour or so before dusk, but not on this day. Entering Messongas Creek, we could see the whitecaps building on the larger water of the Pocomoke Sound. We were thankful for a ride under a leeward bank and a high tide. Our boat ride home was not

Hunting over hand-carved decoys, such as this pair of black ducks, is an experience seldom realized for many hunters. *Jim Lewis photo*.

a long one, but it provided great promise for the day to come. Hundreds of divers, some in small flocks of a dozen, some in flocks numbering fifty or more, lifted off the water in front of our skiff as we made our way back to the ramp. Flock after flock poured into the middle of the creek to raft up for the night. We efficiently got our skiff back on the trailer. We rode in silence back to the shop, both thinking about what lay ahead.

An hour before legal shooting time, we launched our eighteen-foot Gaskill scow and began the short trip to our blind at Deep Hole Gut. My father and I had constructed a comfortable box on the east side of the gut. It was made for three hunters but hunted two much more comfortably. The slightly elevated floor provided dry footing facing the severe high tides brought our way by the strong northeasterly wind. Positioned just on the south side of a small cove, the blind was perfectly situated to attract decoying divers desiring to find shelter from the strong winds. A small gut just on the upwind side of the blind provided the perfect place to stash the boat. Arriving at the blind, I pushed the bow of the boat up on the marsh grass and handed our two guns and shell boxes to my father, my gunning partner for the day. He promptly turned and headed for the box to ready the guns while I haphazardly tossed out a lifelike raft of diver decoys just upwind. With twenty-five decoys in a pile, I let the wind take the boat downwind in front of the blind, trailing a string of divers behind me. With nearly forty decoys bobbing in the wind, I stashed the boat in the small gut and began the fifty-yard walk back to the blind.

With fifteen minutes to spare before legal shooting time, we poured cups of coffee, checked the gun and relaxed as the first of the buffleheads arrived into our little cove. Sipping the coffee, we watched the spirited ducks bounce on the waves. It wasn't long before we had our first opportunity of the day.

Slowly tracking the bank to our left, the pair of black ducks fought to make way against the wind. Their wingbeat paused slightly over the decoys, allowing an excellent shot to start the day. The buffleheads didn't even flinch as the two black ducks hit the water. Both floated with their orange feet flipping in the air. The right-to-left wind combined with a flood tide sent them on a drifting course parallel with the bank. There was no hurry to get the boat in order to retrieve them. They weren't going anywhere, and we'd certainly pick them up in an hour or so. It was now prime time for the divers to begin to fly, but even if they didn't, a pair of black ducks would have made for a satisfactory morning's hunt. Black ducks are big game on Saxis. Local hunters believe that there is a subspecies of black ducks that evolved in the local area. These have a more adept sense of perception and are certainly much smarter than the average bird. I subscribe to this belief.

On the horizon, we began to see flocks of divers beginning to move about. It was clear from the beginning that we were going to have a banner day. I quickly jumped into the boat to retrieve the black ducks before they drifted too far across the creek. With that chore completed, I settled back into the blind as four bluebills circled once, then committed to the "power alley" left in the decoy spread. Poor shooting on our part left only one dead on the water and a second one swimming away fast. Quickly, I made way to the skiff and took off after the crippled bird. He dove as I motored within twenty yards, and I was certain that I hadn't seen the last of him. With my gun shouldered, I knew by experience that he'd surface in about thirty seconds, most likely toward the open water. As his head appeared above the surface, I instinctively fired just over his head, catching him with the bottom of the pattern and not destroying the meat. The drake bluebill was scooped up, along with his band mate, which had drifted just outside the decoys upon my return. I took the opportunity to grab the pair of blacks we'd claimed earlier in the day. By my reckoning, they should have drifted just past the point jutting about two hundred yards from our blind. Leaving the leeward shelter of the bank, the two fat black ducks had been caught in the breeze and were halfway to Tim's Point by the time I caught up with them. Laying them neatly on the seat next to the pair of bluebills, I turned the skiff back into the wind toward the blind. I picked up a single bluebill that my father had capped on the return trip.

Stepping into the box, I was greeted with a hot cup of coffee and a honey bun. Dunking the honey bun in the coffee while gazing toward the open bay, we both felt as though we'd have a couple more opportunities before this hunt was over. That came to light quickly, as a flock of fifty bluebills made the turn around Dick's Point and made their way toward our decoy spread. The fifty flew in wavy lines, low on the water, with designs making their way to the shelter of our little cove. At a distance of one hundred yards, they put twenty yards between them and the water. Their first pass across the decoys was just out of range, but the noise made by the collision of wind and wing was filed permanently in my mind. We watched as they turned in unison, banked into the breeze and circled well outside the decoys.

On their second pass, they meant business. They came in low, and the entire flock fell into the power alley we created in our decoys. We sat there for a minute and watched as they began to make themselves comfortable. Knowing that they would present a small target on the water, we stood together, waiting for them to be tipped off that something was amiss. For a full thirty seconds, they swam and dove, and some began preparation for a

The sound made by the collision of wind and wings is unmistakable. Divers sometimes put on quite an aerial show when decoying in large flocks. *Paul Bramble photo*.

nap until all at once they were startled and rose as one. Six shots rang out, primarily at the mass of fowl and feathers. When all the shooting was over, we expected to see birds everywhere. To our dismay, only a pair lay dead on the water. Our "freezer shot" went terribly awry.

But it's not always the successes that stick in our memory—more often it's the incredible failures. That's one of the oddities about adventure afield. We stood there in disbelief and both started laughing about what had just happened. Expectation certainly didn't meet performance on this occasion. How this had happened we couldn't figure. Tossing our cold coffee over the side of the blind, we refreshed our cups and just stood there in silence thinking about our latest encounter. It was certainly one for the memory.

FINS

Late September can bring some of the best white marlin fishing of the season to Delmarva. Annually, the best of the best converge on our seaside ports to take advantage of huge numbers of billfish congregating in the offshore canyons, from the Wilmington down to the Norfolk, as they feed greedily on their way back south. Though many fish are caught during the tournament season, it's in September when the real numbers are stacked up.

We'd found our fair share just above the Washington and followed them as they moved southward. Fishing with Carey Roberts aboard his White Hot out of Wachapreague, we'd had a couple days with multiple fish but had yet to crack into double digits with a day of ten. The weather and been favorable for two weeks, but a looming northeaster was slated to batter the Eastern Shore over the latter part of the upcoming week. Generally, after a good north blow one of two things will happen. Either it'll school up the bait and the fish, or they'll haul ass out of our fishable range. We waited with anticipation as the storm passed and made plans for a Saturday trip.

On Friday night, we met down at the Wachapreague Marina. While we were rigging baits and listening to the offshore forecast, it looked as if we'd have a decent day. A few beers were consumed, baits were rigged and salted and the general condition of the tackle was reviewed. We went our separate ways, planning on a 5:00 a.m. departure. Not long after that, things began to unravel. By one diversion or another, our crew began to shrink. Five went to four not long after we split up. Sometime around ten o'clock that night, another dropped. The three of us planned on carrying out the plan. Our plan remained to roll on down to the Norfolk.

The next morning, as I walked to the boat, Carey was already on board and had the engines idling. He was certainly excited about our opportunity and was busy fiddling with his electronics. Stowing my gear in the salon, I inquired about the status of our other angler. Carey had heard nothing, and to his knowledge we still had a crew of three. Five o'clock came and went with no sign. Calls to our third's cellphone were unanswered. At 5:20 a.m., we made to the decision to leave without him. Carey would run the boat, and I'd handle the business downstairs. Most likely, this would be our last trip of the season. We'd have to make the most of it.

After we'd cleared the slip and eased out in the channel, I took my coffee to the bridge. The faint pink glow of the coming sun was barely visible on the horizon as we poked the boat's nose in the ocean for the last time of the fishing season. October was a day away, and the extended forecast didn't look good. A series of tropical depressions were lining up to the south, and the mid-Atlantic would most likely not be spared.

The residual seas from our last blow made for a sloppy ride, mostly in the trough, for the duration of our fifty-five-mile trip. Slowing just before our waypoint, I went right to work. The riggers were lowered, and our seven-line spread was quickly deployed. The naked ballyhoo on the flatlines swam magically just outside the prop wash. The bait on the short riggers was dressed with Sea Witches that had been trimmed of about half their hair. Naked baits danced across the surface behind them on the long riggers. Traditionally, we started with a big blue-and-white islander tipped with the biggest bait we could find about two hundred yards behind the boat. It proved effective at picking up stragglers that had a second thought as they drifted out of our spread. We looked good as ever in the three-foot chop.

It didn't take long for the action to begin. Ten minutes into our fishing day, we got jumped by a pack of longfin albacore. As the fifth rod doubled and line began to run off the reel, I began to wonder just what the hell I was going to do with this mess. The first came to the boat nicely, was gaffed and left to bleed all over the cockpit. Two lines went slack simultaneously as they crossed and got chaffed off. A second thirty pounder was brought aboard, and the remaining fish was lost at the leader. We'd been fishing for just under an hour.

For the next twenty minutes, we dealt with the fish we had in the boat. Lines were again set, and we continued our path toward a three-degree change in water temperature. I hoped we'd gotten away from the tunas. Quickly, we found we hadn't, as the port flat line and port long rigger both

Tunas usually arrive to Delmarva waters just ahead of billfish. Local knowledge is key to success, as demonstrated on this trip aboard the *Fishbone. Tom Arnot photo.*

hooked up within three minutes of returning to the water. Another longfin was added to the collection—the second was ignored until it went away.

The next three hours were uneventful. Though warm, the water was an off shade of green and seemingly not conducive to pelagic life. Carey continued to search for better-looking water as I continued to clean tuna blood from the cockpit. Not having the time to deposit the freshly gaffed fish in the confines of a fishbox made cleanup much more difficult. When I was fairly satisfied with the condition of the boat, I went to the galley and produced a pair of Italian subs. Carey and I were enjoying the lunch when something caught his eye ahead and to the starboard. At a distance of two hundred yards, it was unrecognizable. Getting closer, we couldn't believe what we were seeing. Covering a space of nearly an acre was a truly unbelievable site. It appeared to be hundreds of fish, dorsal fins erect, cruising just below the surface. Carey popped to his feet, eyes fixed on what lay before us. I scurried down the ladder, barely touching any rungs, and got ready for action.

At one hundred yards, the number of fins we saw increased dramatically. At fifty yards, they continued to lie just below the surface. At twenty-five yards, it was still hard to fathom. As the boat approached the first of the "fins," a positive identification was made. Pineapples. Dole pineapples. Apparently, they had been blown off a cargo ship during the last storm and sat bobbing around just inside the Norfolk Canyon. Their crowns bobbed in and out of the water, resembling the fins of a school of fish. I began to gaff them as we slowly cruised by and deposited them along the transom. Cutting one open, it was apparent that they were still in great condition. Twenty-two ripe pineapples were added to our catch of longfins.

For the next hour, we trolled with no further activity. The wind began to pick up out of the southwest, and the gray skies began to darken. The decision was made to pull the plug on the fishing day as Casey came off the bridge to start the cleanup of the lines. As the last rod was secured, he disappeared into the salon, returning with a bottle of Meyer's rum and a clean knife. Pineapples cored and juiced. Their husks were transformed into makeshift cups. We hadn't caught our intended species, but the last trip of the year was certainly memorable. The boat drinks were outstanding!

There are smiles all around as a one-hundred-pound swordfish is pulled from the depths off Stuart aboard the *Fishbone*. *Billy Chapman photo*.

IF YOU DON'T GO, YOU'LL NEVER KNOW

Things had been slow throughout the Delmarva region for the third split of the waterfowl season. Puddle ducks few and far between, the only concentration of divers chose to stay north of my latitude and if it wasn't for resident geese, we'd have very few. Interest had begun to wane as several successive trips yielded the same poor results. A Bermuda high dominated our weather for nearly two weeks, providing temperatures more suited for golf than gunning. I fell into somewhat of a duck depression and didn't venture afield for nearly a week. It was the worst of times.

Dedication was being tested as call after call was made to friends from all across the mid-Atlantic who reported the same results. Despite a couple fishing trips and a round of golf or two, it was hard for my soul to reconcile it being gunning season and not going gunning. It wasn't supposed to be this way. It hadn't been this way for forty years, and now all of a sudden I was at a crossroads in my life. Was the interest in fact fading? Was this duck hunting thing that I'd dedicated my life to at an early age something that I was losing interest in? Was it just the lack of birds that was pointing me down this path, or was it something more permanent? Just what the hell was wrong with me?

Peering out of the window of my home office, I could see the sun shining bright as any summer day. The gauge on the thermo unit read forty-eight degrees, with a southwest wind gusting to five. Glancing down at my phone, I could see the time was now 3:49 p.m. A decision had to be made immediately. I decided. What the hell, I hadn't been in a week, so what harm would it be in wasting another hour and fifteen minutes on

Families who work together on the water form tight bonds. Hance and Craig Martin from Saxis exemplified that tradition. *C.L. Marshall photo*.

an otherwise uneventful Tuesday afternoon? Desire outweighed my good sense, and the half-hearted decision was made to give it a go. Quickly, I evaluated the situation. I'd been so disgusted with my last trip that I didn't even unhook the boat from the truck. The goose decoys remained in the boat. I slid into my boots and bibs, donned my coat, grabbed the old double barrel and my gunning bag and was out of the door. I was certain that this hunt wouldn't amount to much, but I remembered our old adage, "If you don't go, you'll never know." The boat was launched at 4:10 p.m., and I began the short five-minute ride to my blind.

Arriving as the sun began to fall quickly in the western sky, I began to arrange fifteen floater goose decoys in what I hoped would be an attractive pattern to passing geese. As the third one splashed in the dark waters of the Pocomoke River, a welcoming sound rang above the din of the idling two-stroke outboard. Turning to the south, a lone honker, with wings spread wide and held motionless, seemingly defied gravity as he glided on a linear path toward my decoys. A single slow, almost growling, honk came from his bill as he passed outside the decoys and slowly continued to make his way up the river. At a distance of forty yards, it would have been a shot worth taking, but the gun was still cased and unloaded as the decoys were being set. I thought of it as a good omen.

It didn't take long to get the last of the fifteen goose decoys in the water, along with a pair of mallards for confidence. This wasn't going to be a long hunt, and I was by myself. I certainly didn't want to have a lot of decoys to deal with. Besides, if it was like the last month, the best part of the hunt would be watching the sun set. As I killed the motor and prepared to set the blind, I heard it again. That same low, guttural noise made only by a goose that had committed to the decoys and was inbound. To the south, along the same line as the visitor that I had just five minutes prior, most likely the same bird was coming back again. Kneeling in the bottom of the boat, I quickly uncased the old Mossberg side by side. Creased the breech and dropped a pair of shells in its chamber and quietly snapped it shut. Still kneeling on the floor of the boat, I glanced up over my right shoulder to see this goose with his feet stretched out just outside the decoys. In a quick, measured motion I swung the bead just in front of the still-moving goose. A single shot from the right barrel left him drifting in the rising tide. A great way to start a short hunt. The blind was set before I reloaded. With just thirty minutes left in this afternoon's hunt, I'd get him on my way out.

The sun shone brightly to my left, and the light south breeze gently sent my mind drifting about the coming of spring and how quickly the winter had passed. Judging from the entries in my logbook, one might think that the season had not been a success. Measured solely by the number of breasts in my freezer, it had been a bust. But this season, more than most, was chock-full of memorable moments. Sitting in the blind atop a full five-gallon bucket, I drifted back in time over the last fifty days. I'd seen my new pup's first retrieve and watched him grow into a dependable retriever. Two had seen me at my absolute worst, screaming like a madman, veins bulging from my neck and face red as fire, with anger directed at this dog that wouldn't stop until he had brought each and every decoy I'd tossed over back to the boat.

I'd again enjoyed an excellent hunt with Steve Barnes and his crew up at the Easton Church of God bash where new friends forged a bond through hunting. On that same trip, I'd removed the shells from the guns of a couple buddies as geese approached decoys and laughed heartily with at the outcome. They returned the favor by dousing the mouthpiece of my goose call with hot sauce during my absence. But the best gag of the day was Steve filling a bag of Combos with dog treats and leaving it open in the blind. Popping a couple in my mouth, I immediately knew that I'd been had but valiantly continued chewing and downed them like nothing was out of the ordinary. I tried, but couldn't hold it in. Those things were disgusting. These are the things that memories are made of.

My thoughts were interrupted by a soft quacking noise to my left. During my hiatus, a pair of mallards had slipped into the decoys unnoticed. It took a second to gather my wits. Peering through the brushes, I gauged them at thirty yards—with the tide coming in my direction, I figured I'd hold off a second in hopes of a better shot. My patience was rewarded as they drifted directly in front of me at twenty-five yards. As the hen brought herself alongside the drake, I capitalized on the opportunity for the two for one. There was little sport in that shot, but this wasn't about the sport; it was about the plate. That pair was destined for Sunday dinner.

Having not risen from my perch atop the bucket, a live shell replaced the spent one. Downriver on the Beverly plantation, the geese that had been feeding greedily in the cut cornfields began to chatter furiously. I'd expected them to return to the river to roost just before dark. It was evident that something, or someone, had startled them, as they all come out at once. Per usual, one could expect smaller groups departing the fields over thirty minutes or so—having them all at once was certainly going to have an impact on my hunting day. It would certainly be over very soon.

Rising and all clamoring at once, a wave of four hundred geese made its way off the fields and crested the loblolly pines that separate the river from the fields. Watching them, I fully expected them to pass to out of range to the south of my little spread. Strung out over the horizon, they continued to make their way toward me. As if I thought it might matter, I laid out a few notes on the Eastern Shoreman for good measure. At an altitude of just thirty yards, the throng continued on a path that would take the birds directly over my spread. Surely this could not be happening. Crouched low and tucked behind the cover of the dark painted fast grass that concealed my little skiff, I watched as the throng showed no signs of changing course. I continued to be pessimistic until the geese reached the far side of the river: at a distance of just 150 yards, the first fifteen set wings in preparation for landing in the decoys. This was going to happen.

At seventy-five yards, the fifteen had doubled in number and continued to glide five or so feet over the calm, dark waters of the Pocomoke River toward my decoys. At thirty yards, the lead gander extended his landing gear and began to slow his forward motion. A single shot accounted for my second goose of the day and filled my legal limit. As if it didn't happen, the remaining geese didn't really flare but just continued on their way up the river one hundred or so yards and set down to roost for the night. I began preparations to do the same.

The birds were retrieved and neatly arranged on the bow. As I began picking up decoys, I thought how the process of hunting was what I seemed to enjoy most about it. I love to watch the birds work, the blue herons searching for minnows in the shallows, the redwing blackbirds

Those who choose not to venture afield in the dead of winter miss many of our region's migratory visitors. *Jim Lewis photo*.

Courtesy Joyce Northam.

soaring overhead in enormous groups spiraling and twisting as if they had one mind. The quiet times allow for thought of what's to come and recollection of what has remained important to us. The misses, the valiant calling that proves unfruitful and the plans that just don't work out are also part of the game. The outcome is never certain, but one thing is for sure.

If you don't go, you'll never know.

LET'S WATCH 'EM

Compared to other gunning seasons that I'd weathered, this one was a good one. Early season was chock-full of locally raised wood ducks blended with early arrivals hastened down our way by several good northeastern blows. Teal followed, making the October split interesting, as our bag was split between blue and green wingers. My Golden, Gunner, was in his prime.

The October split ended, we focused on rockfishing for a bit, but our early success only whet our thirst for the two remaining gunning sessions. Casting bucktails toward ebbing tidal creeks along the edges of the saltwater marshes of the Pocomoke and Tangier Sounds, we watched our number of ducks increase daily. Black ducks were the predominate species, but an increasing number of mallards, teal and baldpates arrived each day. The Thanksgiving split was looking like it was going to be a good one.

As the temps began to cool and the water temps dropped, the divers began to show in earnest. As per usual, the buffleheads and bluebills showed up around mid-November. But rather than just use our waters as a short-term stopover, as the weather turned cold, they elected to stick around for a while. It seems that numbers of ducks attract more ducks. Canvasbacks, redheads and greater and lesser scaup arrived in numbers that we hadn't seen in quite some time. The gunning was fantastic.

The Pocomoke Sound was teeming with waterfowl by Christmas. Thousands of canvasbacks rose from great rafts on the open bay and make a morning trip to the area's muddy bottom to feed on small shellfish and invertebrates. The protected bays provided shelter from the harsh northerly

Called the "King of Ducks" as much for their table value as their decoying ability, canvasbacks hold a revered spot in the heart of many hunters. *Paul Bramble photo.*

winds, making them fine places for these divers to lounge and feed throughout the short winter days. A man could set his watch by them. Each morning and evening, they'd follow almost the same track in their flight plan. The gunning was phenomenal.

Donnie Porter and I had planned to take our sons on a Saturday excursion. The forecast called for northeast winds light in the morning and increasing throughout the day. Parker and I were going to come out of Pitt's Creek, and Donnie's plan was to come from Saxis. We'd found a spot where we'd had consistent action. Our kids, both seniors in high school, had only heard about our exploits and seen the birds in our garages at day's end. They were excited about the opportunity. Gunner was, as usual, always up for the adventure.

Our trip to Double Ditches from Cedar Hall would take about thirty minutes. The sixteen-foot Crestliner was loaded with four-dozen diver decoys, each on individual strings. Donnie's trip was about same, as was his payload. The trip was uneventful but memorable in many ways. The river's surface was smooth as glass, and phosphorescence in the boat's wake could have easily been confused with reflections of the billions of stars that shone brightly overhead. It was a going to be a beautiful Eastern Shore morning.

Parker, Gunner and I arrived at the northern point of Double Ditches before Donnie and Cole. We tossed our gear on the bank and began the task of setting the decoys. We'd been using a traditional J setup with effectiveness for a couple weeks. We set most of our four dozen along the tail of the rig and left a basic framework of the hook for Donnie to fill in. Upon his arrival, he and Cole saw the framework and dutifully got to their task while Parker and I readied our blind. Both the boys had a soccer game at 11:00 a.m., so our hunt would be relatively short-lived, but with any cooperation from the birds, it would be a memorable hunt.

Our blind setup chores were finished just before legal shooting time. A few birds had flickered past our spread in the early-morning light, but we were in no condition to receive them. As Donnie and I stepped into the blind, things immediately began to happen. From the open bay, divers in a long, exaggerated *V*s began to make their way back to the Pocomoke Sound per their daily ritual. At first, they were seen as lines, then individual birds, holding a course along the Maryland-Virginia line. Just past Pig's Point, they began to lose altitude. Hauling a big circle past Flag Pond and Tall Pines and turning hard to the north at Holden's Creek, the first flock of the day would present us with an opportunity. It was a classic bluebill shot. Their first pass outside the decoys resulted in five of the forty landing. The balance of the flock banked hard left toward the open water and began to circle to the decoys.

The second pass would be their last. Falling below the distant tree line, the flock of forty was hard to see in the compromised light. We knew they were coming but not sure of exactly when. Crouched behind the cattails with our guns at the ready, we peered toward the east. At eight yards, we regained contact, and there was no doubt as to what was about to happen. The excitement mounted quickly, turning the next few seconds into what seemed like five minutes. Donnie called the shot perfectly, as most of the birds were over the decoys. When the smoke cleared, bluebills lay floating belly-up, bobbing in the decoys. Two crippled birds swam hard away from the fray.

Gunner didn't see the injured and began his chores. A wing-tipped diver on open bay before sunup is a tall order for any retriever—or person for that matter. We elected to hunt for them in better light. Gunner wasn't a fast swimmer but was very determined in his trade. Two drakes and two hens were delivered to hand and lay across the bow of the boat. Pouring a cup of coffee, Donnie began to chastise us on our lack of shooting skill. From his perspective, we should have limited out on the first pass. We promised to do better and questioned whether or not he had in fact claimed any of our four in the bag.

A single canvasback tried to come in unannounced. Cole spotted him just outside the decoys, wings set and on a slow approach to the hook in the decoys. A fat bull was dispatched in one shot. The morning continued in

Respite in a sheltered cove while the wind whips white the waters of the Chesapeake, a flock of canvasbacks rests in the midday sun. *Paul Bramble photo.*

much the same fashion. It would have been easy to limit out quickly, but we took turns shooting in order increase the harassment quotient on misses. On a falling tide, we had opportunities on blacks, teal, mallards and a lost wood duck. Compliments were seldom handed out. At 8:30 a.m., Gunner and I hopped in the boat and took a look for the wounded divers, finding one.

The main purpose of our ride, however, was to meet my parents at the end of Flag Pond Road. There I picked up a sack of porkchop sandwiches, two Mountain Dews and a Thermos of hot coffee. As I returned to the blind, the weather became absolutely beautiful. The light northeastern wind had fallen out to slick cam, and the sun shone brightly. I parked the boat right in front of the makeshift blind and stepped out onto the firm marsh, passing out sandwiches on the way. There we stood under the bright November sun eating breakfast while watching the decoys do their best to find movement. Parker put his porkchop down on the front of the blind and, with a single shot, sent a decoying hen canvasback to the water. Feet up in the decoys, "Nice shot" was all he got from the rest of our hunting party. Our main focus was on the sandwiches.

With that, we finished our breakfasts and made the decision to pack it in for the day. The boys each had shot a limit of divers, and without any

Quaint fishermen's villages such as Saxis, Virginia, are part of the allure of the Chesapeake. *Jim Lewis photo.*

unforeseen delays, they'd make it to their game on time. Donnie and I elected to meet at 2:00 p.m. for an afternoon hunt. We still had our limits to get. Since it was only three hours away, we left the decoys bobbing. I left my boat pegged to the bank and jumped in with Donnie, and we make our way to Cedar Hall.

Just after two o'clock, Donnie and I stepped into the blind. We flushed a dozen or so birds from the decoys on our approach. That was just a precursor of things to come. We hadn't been in the blind for five minutes when the first pair of bluebills made their way toward our decoys. Three shots left them floating along on the flood tide. Birds came in pairs and threes for the next hour. Choosing our shots well, we slowly inched toward our collective twelve-bird limit. Canvasbacks, redheads, bluebills, teal and mallards made up the pile on the bow of the boat. We were certainly enjoying the afternoon.

We first saw them as they passed over Pig's Point. It looked to be a flock of about eighty following the path that had been followed by flocks of divers in the Pocomoke Sound for decades. Swinging to the east, they followed the shoreline, passing Tall Pines Campground and turning to the north just off Holden's creek. With the wind to their starboard, they traced the edges of the marsh heading toward the mouth of the Pocomoke River and our meager decoy spread. We watched with anticipation as they locked in on our decoys. At a distance of one hundred yards, the entire flock put some distance between themselves and the water, collectively set their wings and made it known that they'd be in our decoys soon.

There was no circling. The entire flock followed the leader and landed just inside the hook of the decoys. Hitting the water, they instinctively began to bunch up. We just watched the event. It would have been easy to shoot in the largest mass of feathers, where dozens would have been killed. Donnie looked over at me and asked the question, "What do you wanna do?" Glancing at the pile of birds we already had, just one shy of our limit, the temptation was there to cut loose. But it just didn't feel right. I answered, "Let's just watch 'em." Donnie just eased back in his seat sipping his coffee and mumbled something under his breath that sounded like, "Jeezus, I've seen it all now." I guess age has a way of tempering the killer in us all.

He continues to remind me of this decision at least once a week.

MAKING SUMPTHIN' OUTTA NUTHIN'

With temperatures dipping into the single digits for nearly two weeks, it was obvious that the Bayside hunting season was all but over. Ten or so days remained in what had been a good season. We'd been steadily working on the geese and a few puddle ducks in the frozen fields, but visions of divers working the icy edges kept bouncing around in my head.

Unverified rumors of open water and bluebills had been the subject of discussion for a couple days. We'd seen good numbers of them flipping around Assawoman Bay near the Veranzanno Bridge on scouting trips to the north, but there was no access up there for us. We figured that if they were up there, they'd be down at Chincoteague. Ripping the top off another Natty Light, we began to hatch a plan for Sunday morning as Parker performed a near-perfect three-point turn before going into the Assateague National Park.

Heading south, we agreed that we'd take Krabill's fiberglass boat. It was heavier, had more power and looked to be in better late-season condition that our Carolina skiff. Additionally, the semi-V hull would bust through the thick ice where the lighter skiff would simply slide on top of it, leaving us stranded with just the prop in the water. Cruising down to the Greenbackville harbor, we all felt as though that would be our optimum place of launch to provide us access to the throngs of ducks working the edges of the open water about halfway to Chincoteague. Though the ramp was iced in, and there was ice as far as we could see, we figured that we'd find open water near the mouths of some of the swift-running guts that had yielded topwater redfish just five months prior. With

For many, ice in the Chesapeake closes their season. For those who hunt diving ducks, it's just what they're looking for. *Jim Lewis photo.*

that, I circled through the harbor parking lot, and the three of us, Kyle, Parker and myself, headed to the barn to ready for the coming adventure.

Back at the barn, several bags of diver decoys were tossed in the boat and the gas tanks topped off. Gunning bags were packed, a pair of Thermoses was prepped with hot water and the guns were oiled and sleeved. Six geese and six each of blacks and mallards were added the mix. To add a degree of authenticity to the spread, I added eight field mallards that we would use to stand on the ice. It seemed like a very good plan. With a nod, we went our separate ways.

Waking thirty minutes before the alarm, I was quickly dressed, and the smell of brewing coffee brought Parker downstairs in a trancelike state a few minutes later. With virtually all the prep done the evening before, there was little to do but collect what little bit of gear was outstanding and make our way to Krabill's. Just after five o'clock, we began the treacherous twelve-mile ride over the snow- and ice-covered back roads. We were in no hurry, as our plan was to launch with the rising sun.

As the straps were being removed from the boat, I glanced at the ice in the launch ramp. With that, I bid farewell to the LED lights on the trailer.

Certainly, they would be destroyed by the thick ice as the boat was backed in to the ramp. Kyle just laughed with his usual comment, "Man, I just can't have nothing!"

With a little jockeying, the trailer and boat finally found open water below the broken ice. The trailer was parked, and we began the task of getting the boat turned and heading out of the marina. It was more of a task than we had anticipated. Just forty yards from our launch, the five-inch-thick ice proved too thick for our boat to break. Our trench we had broken had all but closed up, and we were stuck. There was no way to turn around, and reverse wouldn't yield enough propulsion to provide any headway. We weren't going anywhere.

With a little discussion, we hatched a plan we thought would get us, and the boat, back to the dock. Kyle simply stepped off the boat and walked across the ice back to the dock. Our plan was to unhook the trailer from the truck, fashion a tow rope and use the truck to pull us back to the ramp. As the truck backed down the ramp, I walked across the ice to grab the tow rope. Once both ends were attached, the boat was pulled back toward the ramp stern first. Turning the boat around to be able get it back on the trailer would require a little redneck engineering. We simply ran the tow rope around the offside piling as the truck pulled away. The bow of the boat slid around nicely. With the trailer reattached, the boat was loaded. As the trailer was pulled clear of the ice, I noticed the crushed red lenses of the trailer lights stuck in the ice and was sure to make mention of it. Kyle just shook his head and jumped in the truck.

Dropping the boat back at Camp Krabill, we tossed some gear in the back of the truck, topped off our coffees and took off to find open water. Sitting in the truck at Red Hills, we noticed several flocks of puddle ducks huddled on the ice. With some regularity, small flocks of birds would materialize and join the throng. After watching for twenty or so minutes, we decided that we'd give it a try. With guns, a box of shells and our eight decoys in tow, we walked across Swan Gut toward the fowl on the ice. We found an old launch boat for cover and set out our small spread.

Things got underway quickly as a group of six geese made their way along the frozen shoreline toward our position behind the beached boat. With no goose decoys, we didn't figure on having much of a chance, but Parker's calling grew in intensity. Glancing out from behind our cover, I could see that we were going to have a chance. With the snow beginning to fall, the six dropped below tree level out of the harsh northwest wind. As if on cue, Parker's calling became more sensuous as the six simultaneously set

On a recent Thanksgiving hunt with my sons, Hunter and Parker, three decoying geese made memories that we'll not soon forget. This huge goose was destined for dinner later that day. *C.L. Marshall photo.*

their wings and began to glide toward our sparse rig. There'd be no circling, and we rose in unison as the six got within thirty yards. Three fell to the ice with our first volleys, subsequent shots claiming only one more. The two survivors quickly climbed above tree level and were carried out of danger by the twenty-knot northwestern wind.

Walking out on the ice to pick up the geese, we noticed several flocks of geese to our south on the ice. Flock after flock of ducks fell into them while we watched. Returning to our makeshift blind, we discussed our observations and decided to grab a dozen or so goose decoys from the barn. Within thirty minutes, we had collected the decoys, traversed the ice-covered creek and found our way back to our spot. The decoys were placed close together on the ice similar to the ones half mile to our south. Within minutes, our decision to make the change paid dividends, as twenty gadwalls with bowed wings hung over the goose decoys. We performed nicely.

As we were celebrating our good fortune, Kyle spotted four black ducks low over the ice. A strong hail call followed by a few urgent quacks was all that was required to close the deal. Three of the four did as expected and joined our bag. The fourth never really came in range and escaped unscathed.

Extended periods of cold drive waterfowl south. Perseverance made the taking of these banded birds possible in frigid conditions. *C.L. Marshall photo.*

Birds were everywhere. Flocks of blacks, gadwalls and mallards crisscrossed the ice and tree line. Fifteen widgeon fell out of the stratosphere and were held motionless as they stemmed the wind just twenty yards above the decoys. As we rose to shoot, they quickly flared. Parker and I connected. Kyle's pump failed to fire the first shot; his second claimed the lone gadwall in the bunch.

The morning continued as we celebrated our good shots, heckled one another for our misses and collectively shared a memorable morning. Within short order, our limit was reached and we were sipping hot coffee in the truck back on the way to warm ourselves around the wood stove. My day was done as I headed for work on an afternoon perfect for gunning. Parker and Kyle pummeled them again in the afternoon as I pecked away at my keyboard. Pictures and Snapchats regularly interrupted my Sunday chores.

Our day could have easily ended after our morning miscues. It would have been easy to cash it in and head for the warmth of home. Having a no-quit attitude and ability to change plans quickly based on the day we were given turned a busted hunt into a very memorable day. We certainly made something outta nothing.

A MARLIN PRICK

For the aspiring fisherman, the Eastern Shore of Virginia is an excellent choice for a place to live. The options seem endless, and often failure occurs from one not being able to decide between the myriad choices at one's disposal. But for us, one weekend in late July was always marked in pen on the calendar. The Eastern Shore Marlin Club's annual tournament was something that we always looked forward to.

During its heyday, the ESMC tourney fielded a fleet of over seventy boats, many electing to stop and fish on their way up the coast to Ocean City for the "big money" tournaments. Some elected to fish from Virginia Beach, others from Chincoteague. Winning fish, however, must be weighed in Wachapreague. During that time, the marina bustled with activity. There were no fewer than a dozen offshore charter boats, that number or more private boats and a host of inshore charter options all busily handling customers from all across the mid-Atlantic. Three restaurants fed the visitors, and rooms at the Wachapreague Hotel were booked long in advance of the tournament. It was a very cool place to be.

We entered every year, more for the camaraderie and the experience than anything else. It was a fairly inexpensive way to fish a three-day tournament with friends. Our usual carriage was a diminutive Mako 224 powered by a single 225 Yamaha. It wasn't big. It wasn't fancy. But in it our team of Paige Linton, Rick Beardmore and myself felt as confident as the big Oceans and Vikings that ran from other ports. But this particular year, the Mako was out of service due to an issue with the big Yamaha. We elected to enter with

Beardmore's boat, a refinished 233 Formula with a new Volvo 350 that was barely broken in. The name on the boat fit him well, *Insatiable*. In the weeks and days prior to the tournament, we prepped the boat, making certain that we had solutions to each possible scenario that might occur. I'd never fished on the boat, but I knew friends who ran similar hulls and they confirmed in moderate seas it would perform well.

The fishing had been a little on the slow side, and that dominated the discussion at the traditional Thursday night kickoff dinner. Now this dinner alone was worth the price of the entry fee. It was a true delight to find tables filled with steamed crabs and clams, corn, oysters and fried chicken. All of the best of the Eastern Shore was lovingly prepared and served with that typical Eastern Shore of Virginia flair. Food and friends were abundant as plans were made for fishing two out of the upcoming three days. Our plan was to lay in on Friday and fish back-to-back days on Saturday and Sunday. With that decision made, we proceeded to relax and have a few extra beverages on a wondrous Wachapreague evening.

The night's activities prompted a late wakeup call on Saturday morning. Sluggishly, we showered and made our way across the street to the tackle shop, where hot coffee got our day underway. The wind was from the southwest at fifteen miles per hour, occasionally gusting to twenty, and forecasted to drop

A leaping blue marlin is a wonderful sight to see, but at boatside, they can be a very dangerous opponent. *Jake Graves photo.*

off in the afternoon hours. Light and variable winds were called for on each Saturday and Sunday. We agreed that we'd made the right decision. The day was used to get the boat in its slip, rig baits and finish up any unfinished business that would be required over the weekend. Loran coordinates were plugged in for where we thought we'd be heading, plus others for secondary and tertiary locations. Our collective effort and our unpressured pace made the preparation enjoyable. By midafternoon, we had the boat rigged and ready for action. We retreated to the Island House for a late lunch and cold beer as we waited for the few who went fishing today to return. Information gleaned from them would be vital in making our decisions for the coming day. Few fish were caught the first day. We hatched a plan based on the best information we could glean from a variety of sources. After a few leisurely cocktails after dinner, we retired for the evening. The next two days would be long and full. Or so we hoped.

The day dawned as we passed the C buoy out of Wachapreague. The seven-mile trek to the inlet had been a slow process following the larger offshore battlewagons, which draw much more water than our little Formula. Once outside the inlet, we set the cruise at twenty-seven knots for a waypoint about halfway between the Washington and Poor Man's Canyons. The seas had a gentle swell from the southwest, and the wind, what there was of it, provided little ripples on the surface. The weather had certainly cooperated, and for once, the weatherman had it right. We felt confident we'd find a yellowfin tuna or two, but our sights were on white marlin.

The ride out was uneventful. Rick pulled the throttle back at 8:15 a.m. as the old Ray Nav 580 chirped, noting our arrival at our predetermined waypoint. Per tournament regulations, fishing wasn't permitted to begin for another fifteen minutes. The baits were made ready, outriggers deployed, as we idled patiently looking for the perfect place to be when the call for line in was broadcast by a committee boat. We could hear the normal radio chatter, and we could tell that most of the fleet had ventured south toward the Norfolk and just below the Washington. It appeared that aside from a few Ocean City boats, we'd have the area to ourselves.

The call came, and we quickly and efficiently began to get our gear out. We ran skirted ballyhoos on the long riggers, larger skirted horse ballyhoos on the short riggers and naked small baits on the flat lines. Our center rigger, or way, way, way, back bait was positioned fifty yards behind our longest offering. The long and short rigger baits weren't rigged with traditional monofilament leaders but rather single strand 80# coffee-colored wire. These four mylar-adorned Sea Witches had caught numerous whites, tunas and dolphin for us to date. This was no time to change what had been working for us thus far.

Our first bite occurred about an hour into the day. A single white appeared behind the port flat line with pectoral fins lit up in bright cobalt blue. Rising from under the bait, I watched as his dorsal broke the surface and his bill swatted at what he thought would be an easy breakfast. Popping the line free from the flatline clip, the bait fell perfectly into this open mouth. Resisting the urge to set the hook prematurely is key to getting tight on billfish. With the reel in free spool, the line left the reel at an accelerated pace. It was evident that he had the bait as I pushed the lever drag of the TLD 25 to strike. We called in the first hook up of the tournament.

The drag did its job, and the barb buried in the fish's jaw. I passed the rod to Paige and waited for a minute or so before clearing the other lines. Seeing no other customers, the other six lines were quickly cleared as the battle ensued. Twenty minutes later, I secured the leader and had the fifty-pound white by the bill. After a few quick pics, the fish was released unharmed. A release time was duly recorded by the committee boat and on our catch report. Quickly, we reset the lines with hopes at an all-time high.

Johnny Morris and guests pose aboard the *Fishbone* with a nice daytime sword plucked from the Florida coastal waters. *Tom Arnot photo.*

Hunting and Fishing by the Tides

As the day wore on, we stayed in the same general area and scratched two more whites out of four bites. Radio contact was spotty throughout the day, but on the way in, it became obvious that we'd be tied with another boat going into the final day of fishing. Knowing that ties would be broken in the second day by the first fish caught and released, we discussed our plan for the second day. We felt that our piece of water held a few fish but was moving south quickly. Our plan was to move south with it, starting just above the Washington in about fifty fathoms.

Day three dawned just like its predecessor, and we again found ourselves rigged and ready for the call for "lines in." Right along the fifty curve, in the vicinity of a line of lobster balls with "Toots" spray-painted on them, was some of the prettiest water that any marlin fisherman could ask for. A dozen or so Ocean City boats had been fishing for a bit, but we had heard of none caught by the time that day three began.

Just after nine o'clock, we noticed some activity on the surface near an approaching lobster ball. Passing it on the inshore side, the source of the commotion was soon evident. The sickle-like dorsal fin was unmistakable. It didn't have the gentle rounding of a white. The small blue marlin accelerated swiftly toward the green and yellow Sea Witch, which ran just ahead of a swimming horse ballyhoo on the shortrigger. It didn't miss its mark as the bait was inhaled just prior to thrashing across the surface of the ocean for a hundred yards or so. Rick was standing beside the rod as the whole event took place. With the rod in his hands and Paige at the helm, we began to track this beast down. The fight didn't take long. Within four minutes, I had secured the leader and the official release called in. Still a little green at boatside, the fish darted under the boat and I pushed the wire leader around the transom but couldn't get it around the outdrive quickly enough. In the millisecond that it took to attempt to free the leader, the fish turned and accelerated again toward the port side of the boat. As it emerged from under the boat, I clearly saw the 125-pound marlin's eye fixed on what appeared to be me. His anger was evident, and I'm sure he had plans to do me as much harm as possible to ensure his escape. As the leader came tight, the fish exited the water, coming back toward the cockpit much like a yo-yo on a tight string. This fish was inbound, and I ducked in an attempt to get out of harm's way, but it was too late. Striking me solidly in the arm with its bill, the fish and I tussled for a bit on the engine box. After what seemed like an eternity, but in reality was only about five seconds, the fish was pushed across the transom and was back in his element.

Handling a large fish at the boat often requires breaking out the heavy gear to finish the game. There's nothing quite like a well-placed harpoon shot. *Billy Chapman photo.*

Blood was everywhere in the cockpit. Some of it belonged to the marlin, and undoubtedly some of it was mine. With the adrenaline pumping, I knew that I'd been hit but wasn't exactly sure where or how badly. The answer came instantly as I tried to get up off the engine box. My left arm had gone numb from the impact. A deep puncture wound in my shoulder oozed blood and slime. It hurt like hell.

We quickly went through all the gauze and isopropyl alcohol that we had on board. After ten or so minutes, we had the bleeding under control and began to access just how bad this injury was. The arm wasn't broken, and the shoulder, though sore, wasn't dislocated. It just hurt like no other. Rick was down below looking for additional first aid gear as Paige applied pressure and tried to clean the wound. The only additional first aid equipment that Rick could produce was an unopened quart of Jim Beam. It worked wonders for the pain and moderately well as an antiseptic.

After a few nips off the bottle, I decided that the injury wouldn't get any worse over next few hours. I'd relinquish my position in the cockpit in exchange for a seat at the wheel and the remainder of the bottle of Beam. We fished along for the next few hours, picking up a pair of gaffer dolphin and a fat yellowfin tuna. Nearing two o'clock, we decided to head for the inlet. At the dock, we were met by a team of paramedics who surveyed the wound and did their best to clean it. A visit to the emergency room provided the required shots and prescriptions for infection control. I'm sure that the medical staff was glad to see me leave due to my intoxicated state. I've been told it was quite comical.

That fourth fish sealed the win for the *Insatiable* team in dramatic fashion. Though many billfish had been caught before and after that small blue, it's still the one that sticks out in my mind as the nastiest. I've got the scars to prove it.

NATURAL LIGHT FLU

It was the day that we had waited several years for. Heavy snowfall to the north and a strong Arctic Clipper had pushed a tremendous amount of waterfowl to the Eastern Shore in search of food and open water. Geese, canvasbacks, bluebills and puddle ducks of all sorts were invading our local waters by the thousands. Hunting was as good as it could get.

The front moved southward, and the temperatures dropped. As the Bay began to freeze, we were treated with some of the finest field hunting we've had in years. As we lay in our layout blinds, mallards formed tornado-like funnels as they swirled overhead. Black ducks, widgeons and wood ducks made regular appearances to pick up spilled grain as the marshes became more inhospitable. As we were picking up our rig after a quick afternoon hunt, we watched flock after flock of puddle ducks fall into the Pocomoke River. With the rig properly stowed in the enclosed trailer, we started a little exploration. It was better than we could ever have imagined.

The smaller finger creeks and freshwater ponds were the first to freeze, pushing the hordes of new birds out to the larger, wind-whipped waters of the Pocomoke Sound. Two days later, the Bay was covered with ice. Yet the swift current of the Pocomoke River kept the ice at bay. A small crust adorned the pockets protected from the river's flow, but the river remained open. The ducks literally flocked to it. My gunning partner, Kyle Krabill, and I hauled our stuff home and began making preparations for the next day's adventure. We stopped by the Goose Creek for some Fatty Nattys on the way to the shop. We quickly unloaded our gear into the garage and quickly hooked up the gunning skiff. Inside the garage, we gave our guns the once over.

Popping open the first beers of the evening, we began to go through our gunning bags. Shells, calls, gloves, secondary gloves, dip, flashlights and all the other necessary items were checked. Another beer and we began loading decoys in the boat. Eighteen GHG Canada goose floaters, a dozen mallards and another dozen black ducks were packed into front part of the sixteen-foot Alumacraft. The Marshall Custom Pop Up blind was checked for adequate cover, and two panels of fast grass were added for good measure. The fuel tank was topped off with gas and oil, and we were quickly back inside the garage. A few more beers were tipped as the remainder of the next day's supplies were readied and we parted ways. A reunion was scheduled for 5:15 a.m. at the usual spot.

Rolling up to the convenience store at 5:20, I could see that Krabill was already there. Parking the truck in the middle of the lot, I immediately headed in for coffee. Rather than load his stuff in the boat, Krabill slowly found his way out of his F-250 and followed me into the store. Armed now with a full Thermos, a cup of coffee apiece and a custard-filled Tasty Klair, I was beginning to be ready to face the day. Krabill didn't say much as he loaded his gear into the boat. As he hopped into the truck and took a long pull off his coffee, it was clear to see that his night had been similar to mine. Exchanging stories of our evenings on the way to the boat ramp, it was clear that neither of us were exactly "on top of our game."

Dwindling Canada goose populations have called for a reductions in harvest. The resident population remains strong. *Jim Lewis photo.*

Having circled the sun nearly forty times since I was deemed legally of age to consume spirits, I'd overindulged several times. The cold air of the boat ride, a couple cups of java and a little physical activity were usually all that were required to get things back on an even keel. Today, I thought, would be no different.

The short boat ride went as expected. Kyle and I selected a good place to tuck the boat and began the task of setting the decoys. The geese were gingerly placed so as not to splash water on their sides and back. Positioned more toward the middle of the river, and just a little upwind, the eighteen went out without incident. Inshore and downwind, the ducks were placed in the shallowest of water and in a pile. We wanted them to show up as a feeding mass of waterfowl. The haphazard method achieved that goal fairly well.

With the boat in place and the blind popped up, we were ready for action. Uncasing our guns and readying our shell boxes, an untold number of teal zipped just atop the tall reeds to our back and settled into the goose decoys without circling. Having just over fifteen minutes to legal shooting time, we just kept at our task as the teals' shrill whistles broke the morning silence. We each poured another cup of coffee. The teal left immediately after the Thermos slipped from my hand and hit the bottom of the boat.

We sat sipping coffee and witnessed the marsh come to life. No two times are alike. The raspy predawn locator calls from hen mallards and black ducks filled the air. Band-tailed hawks and bald eagles silently stalk in the low light, looking for any advantage they can get. With low, direct flight, wood ducks make their way from their nighttime haunts in the cypress swamps toward more suitable feeding areas. Owls, turkeys and marsh hens each make their presence known as the sun creeps toward the horizon. As the hour of reckoning draws near, we become increasingly aware of each creature. Each day is different. Each day is the same.

The phone dinged, signaling the legal beginning of another hunting day. Ducks were in the air everywhere in flocks of six, ten, fifteen and too many singles to keep up with. A poor effort at a highball caught the interest of six mallards that immediately lost altitude, crossed the point to our left and turned into the stiff northwest wind. They seemed to hang motionless over the decoys, their forward progress thwarted by the wind and cup of their wings. The oyster-white feathers of the interior of their wings flashed in the first few rays of the sun as it prepared to peek over the horizon. Finding our feet, we unleased six shots toward the unsuspecting fowl. Somehow, we managed to rag a single hen out of that flock. Cussing our poor shooting, we reloaded just as three blacks locked up in the heavens and fell toward the decoys at a rapid pace. Six more shots were unleased prior to two escaping unscathed.

A little discussion followed about what had just occurred. Under normal circumstances, we'd have whacked those two blacks and picked up at least three of those mallards. A few motivational phrases were exchanged, another cup of coffee poured and the Tasty Klairs uncased. It was clear that we'd have more chances, and it was time to get with the program.

Coming from the Beverly marsh, two wood ducks lost a little altitude and sidestepped the wind as the outside edge of our decoys. Four more shots yielded nothing. A single mallard provided an excellent opportunity, yet we failed to draw a feather.

Looking at Kyle, I instructed him to case his gun. This had gone on long enough. Casing our guns, we prepared to pick up the decoys, which was done in short order. The boat was back on the trailer by 8:15 a.m. We discussed our issues, our misgivings from the night before, and agreed to get our shit together and meet at noon. We headed directly for Market Street Deli and a couple scrapple, egg and cheese sandwiches. Scrapple is a magical meat. Kyle was deposited at his truck, mine left at the curbside, and my ass found a familiar spot on the sofa, where I remained until 11:30 a.m.

As I ambled toward the kitchen for another cup of coffee, things were beginning to become a little more in focus. Picking Kyle up, I could see that the break had served him well. We embarked on our afternoon adventure. Arriving at the dock, it was plain to see that this was going to be one to remember. There were ducks everywhere.

Courtesy Joyce Northam.

The boat was again quickly launched. Our heads were on the swivel on the boat ride back to our appointed spot. Puddle ducks were everywhere. Mallards, blacks and teal lined the shallow shorelines. Bluebills and Cans cut down the center of the river. Geese shuttled from the freshwater river back to the adjacent fields. Quickly we set up and were back in business. Soon enough, we found that our fates had changed greatly.

Five mallards hooked over the point to our left and immediately fell toward our spread. Four shots rang out, and a fifth was saved as the sole survivor made a hasty exit. As we were chatting about our new beginning, Kyle rose on instinct. A drake wood duck, in full plumage, was added to the pile.

We picked and chose our shots at ducks to fill out our limits to their maximum potential. Our shooting improved greatly, as did our enjoyment of the day's events. Several flocks of twenty-plus geese landed and were flushed away. We prolonged our time in the blind by taking our four-goose limit from decoying two singles and a pair of geese that made their minds up from half a mile in the stratosphere.

With our colorful limit displayed on the bow, we sat with unloaded guns watching the show. It was the perfect storm of Pocomoke River duck hunting. The bay was frozen, the fields were full and the only strand of open water was the swift-running ribbon where we were hunting. Birds shuttled back and forth between field and our decoys for the hour we sat watching the show.

Having successfully survived our bout with the Natural Light Flu we found our afternoon groove. With proper execution and a little rest, it was much more of what we expected. Actually, it was a lot more than that.

OLD PAINT

The prior year's hunting season had ended rather abruptly. Hunting hadn't been that great, and the decoys were washed and quickly put in storage containers to rest until the upcoming season. The grind of gunning several days on end had been difficult. The birds had been few and far between, and I was somewhat glad that my season was going to come to its end a week early.

Boarding the plane, I had visions of Costa Rican sailfishes dancing on the end of my line. That sure sounded better than staring off into the birdless skies, which had occupied the prior my two weeks. The vacation came and went, as did the summer. Spring trout fishing moved quickly into fall rockfishing. Ultimately, as surely as the changing of seasons along the mid-Atlantic, my interests turned to the coming hunting season.

The beginning of each season beams with new promise. With each passing year, the preparation becomes increasingly gratifying. Age may have something to do with that. Pulling the decoys off the shelves from where they sat stacked in storage totes over the summer, I removed each for inspection. The differences in like models could be seen by only me. The newer ones would have their lines and weights checked, knots removed from their lines and then neatly stacked back in their containers. The newer foam-filled decoys should provide years of use with minimal maintenance. A touch of paint here and there after a few years and they should be good to go. The older the decoy, the more work it'll require. Younger hunters might just opt to replace the older dekes with newer ones. But for an old-

A knife in the hands of a skilled carver can yield decoys that will become family treasures. *Jim Lewis photo.*

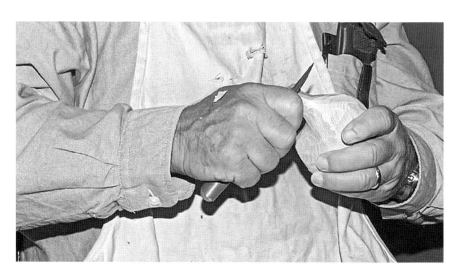

The character the carver instills into each of his decoys is part of the allure for collectors and the success of those who hunt over them. *Jim Lewis photo.*

school duck hunter, that's not the case. There's certainly a time when this step becomes necessary, but the new dekes lack the character developed from countless trips.

Decoys gain this character in many ways. Bouncing around in the bottom of a gunning skiff crossing the rough waters of Rehoboth Bay is a good start to decoys adding this intangible allure. A stray shot here and there contributes as well. General wear created by use is just that—general wear. It's the details and individual characteristics developed by years, and sometime decades, of use that makes certain decoys special.

The tote full of Herter's Canada goose floaters was pulled beside the table, and the remaining six decoys were placed gingerly in two rows. These full-body decoys were unique in their construction. Fashioned out of one piece of thick plastic, their heads and keel were molded in with the body. They were among the first to be filled with expanding foam and have stood the test of time. These six are the remnants of a rig that my uncle Danny Marshall had used at the Fox Island Gun Club in the 1960s. They had been given to my father when he began to take me hunting in the 1970s. Now these half-dozen fifty-year-old decoys bob alongside their newfangled cousins. One guest called them a spread "filler." I think of them as the center of my rig. The rest is just filler to me. They've earned their spot. The new ones still have work to do.

Over the years, the rig has taken some casualties. Dogs and kids have scampered over them in the boat, snapping off several heads. T shot has riddled the bodies of several past the point of recovery. But these six remain. Scarred, scratched and strafed by years in the line of fire, they now sit atop the work bench begging not to be made new again but, rather, to again be used. The repairs will only dress up the outward appearance, not add to their character. Not unlike pigs and lipstick.

Scraping off the peeling paint, thoughts of preseason prep in years gone by come to mind. The layers of paint on these old geese go back decades. I'd painted these same decoys with my father. He took the time to show me how to blend the paint to get just the right muted tone of burnt umber for the back. I'd done the same with my sons, and together we'd killed our fair share of geese over these old decoys.

Countless friends have hunted over these decoys with me. Though their lot in life may have changed, these decoys are reminders of the hours shared in the blind. As the chips of paint fell on the table, memories continued to come. Starting to scrape them away, I couldn't help but think of the memories that each layer represented. In their prime, they had seen many

An old, worn mallard decoys warms in the morning rising sun. Old decoys have a story, a history, that their newer counterparts have yet to earn. *Paul Bramble photo.*

northeasters behind the bar at Fox Island Gun Club. A layer of paint or two later, they'd witnessed Lou Spence take five widgeon on the wing in three shots at Bombay Hook. They'd sat idle for nearly a decade until they found their way to me. Within those layers that I added, they'd witnessed me at my best and at my worst. They'd seen five good gun dogs that I trained swim by fetching fooled fowl. My father, I and both my sons had grabbed them by the head and tossed them in the waters of Cattail Creek. Layers upon layers of memories began to run through my mind, each unlocked as the layers of paint were exposed.

I can remember my first goose falling among the floaters. Both my sons and countless friends found success in various forms in their presence. These old one-piece wonders of mass production had long outlived their anticipated life expectancy, but they still had much to offer.

Reluctantly, the old paint was scraped off, a light sanding applied, then recoated with new colors. They stand out from the rest of my rig. The size and paint don't exactly match the new GHGs. Therein lies the beauty of these six. They're different. They're old. They've earned their spot in my heart and in my rig. Their newer cousins may never be held in the same regard.

REDNECKS IN THE DOVE FIELD

Growing up in Sanford, Virginia, there were many hunting opportunities. Ducks and geese were regulars on the docket. Deer were plentiful, and there always seemed to be one in the freezer. Small game was occasionally taken, but most of our time was spent chasing game that would fill the center of the plate. Doves were not something we had opportunity to hunt. That all changed with a call from Ronnie Kellam.

I knew Ronnie, as he was a lower shore farmer and a supporter of our high school's athletic program. He, and many like him, made sure that we had what we needed to keep our programs running. Ronnie and my father worked tirelessly to this end. Opening day of dove season fell on a Saturday, and we graciously accepted his invitation to join him and numerous other kindred spirits for an afternoon of dove hunting, barbecue and cold beer at one of his seaside farms on the Accomack/Northampton county line. It was an opportunity we couldn't refuse.

Neither Dad nor I had ever participated in an organized dove hunt such as this. We wouldn't be brandishing the newest over/under shotguns; instead, we oiled up our Browning Automatics, removed the rings and donned our best cattail camo and headed south. Arriving at the farm, we were greeted by many familiar faces and some damn good barbecue. After sharing fellowship and a couple sandwiches, our attentions turned to hunting. With a little cloud cover, temperatures in the mid-fifties and a light northeastern wind, it was a great day for hunting. While feasting and waiting on the noon start time, we witnessed a field filled with feathered targets. Some flying in singles and pairs, others in groups of twenty-five or more, twirled around the field feeding and intermittently roosting in the loblolly pines that bordered the field on three sides. The east side was bordered by a slim thread of marshland that separated the field from the Machipongo River.

With lunch about to wrap up, we began to make preparations to take to the field. We asked Ronnie where we should venture to, and he pointed to a pair of pine trees located near the middle of the corn stubble. He said it would be about as good a place as any. With that, Dad and I began the couple-hundred-yard trek across the field to take our positions. Upon arrival, we immediately loaded our guns and waited for the stroke of high noon. Precisely at that hour, shooting began. Somewhat slowly at first, the shooting then built steadily in volume over the course of the first hour. A light mist began to fall from the sky as single birds began to make their way to our little stand on a repetitive basis. We'd take turns and usually back each other up.

Bobby Graves holds a shallow water redfish caught near the Machipongo River. *C.L. Marshall photo.*

Not all memorable fish are huge. This small speckled trout caught by Max Finzano highlighted a memorable trip. *C.L. Marshall photo.*

From the shooting standpoint, we approached it like any other duck hunt. The shots were fairly easy for the experienced dove hunter, but for us, each time we pulled the trigger it was in hope that the bird would dart in front of the shot. Our misses equaled our hits for the first hour.

As the birds began to fly with regularity, we could hear our fellow hunters shouting some kind of communication. Being nearly one hundred yards from the nearest hunter, we could hear the sounds but couldn't make out what they were saying. It sounded like "AAAARRRRFFFF," but we couldn't be sure. Our shooting improved as the number of birds seeking food increased. As a flock of four slowed for landing in the tree we were standing over, Dad let out a loud "AAARRRFFF!" as he began on the left side of the foursome and worked right. I met him in the middle as four fell to the ground. All I could do was laugh.

From that point on, it wasn't really a fair fight. Two old school duck hunters with automatic weapons standing in a cornfield under a pair of pines certainly tipped the odds vastly in our favor. Our shooting had improved greatly as flocks of ten to fifteen birds became the norm. It wasn't long before we reached our fifteen-bird-each limit. After collecting our birds and policing our shell casings, we began to make our way out of the field. Ronnie was on his way toward us as we began our exit. In passing, he congratulated us on our good luck. I asked inquisitively what he and the other hunters were yelling at one another. "Oh, you mean, 'Mark,'" he said. I asked, "What the hell was that for?" He answered, "To let each other know of approaching birds." Dad and I just laughed as our dove hunting vocabulary increased.

I returned to that same field some years later to hunt mallards and geese. The pines we stood under were still there and had grown many feet taller. While there, I thought often about the late Ronnie Kellam in hopes that he too found as much humor in that day as we did. While in our blind that day, I could still hear us yelling, "AAAARRRFFFFF!" and whaling away at the doves as they tried to find the safety of the pines. It's the stuff good hunts are made of.

RINGBILLS

It was one of the worst duck seasons that the Eastern Shore had ever weathered. The early-season teal were here and gone before the season opened. The hatch of wood ducks was off, and the migratory population of wood ducks was pushed out due to a couple of rather severe tropical depressions. The weather was much too mild for divers, and there was little interest in hunting the few sea ducks that hung on the bars in the Pocomoke Sound.

It was not a good year, but we're duck hunters. We go anyway. And that is precisely what Fred Vaughn and I planned to do on a sunny Saturday afternoon. After a garage lunch of rockfish sandwiches and steamed clams, we loaded the boat with an odd mix of decoys and began to make our way down to the ramp. The plan was to spend a leisurely afternoon grilling sandwiches, reheating crab soup and enjoying the outdoor Delmarva scenery. Ducks were going to be a bonus, if there were any.

Leaving the house, we planned to launch at Cedar Hall, but after a bit of a quick diversion we altered our plan and made our way to Pitt's Creek. Our plan was to set up in Bull Beggar Creek in hopes of picking off a local black duck, a lost goose or possibly a pair of fat mallards. The way the season was going, there was little likelihood of that, but with hopes high, Fred, Milo and I piled in the little aluminum skiff and made our way out of the mouth of the Pocomoke and around to the mouth of the first creek to the left. Setting up in a slight widening of the creek with a small exposed mudflat to our left, we somewhat liked our chances. Twenty or so divers

Cold, windy weather is perfect for those pursuing canvasbacks on the open waters of the Chesapeake. *Paul Bramble photo*.

were set in the traditional *J* pattern in front and a little upwind of our selected spot. Fifteen blacks, mallards and teal were haphazardly tossed inside and downwind of the divers.

The breeze gusted out of the north, sometimes raging up to eight miles per hour. Most of the time, it hovered at a brisk three to five. The sun shone brightly in a crisp blue winter sky as we poured hot coffee from our rusty green Stanley Thermos. It was not the perfect hunting day, but it wasn't really about the prospect of laying a smackdown on a pile of greenheads. This afternoon was about reconnecting with a friend; hunting was just the setting to make it happen. Under bluebird skies, we stood in the blind and spent the time reconnecting. Under duckless skies, we admittedly lost interest in the hunting endeavor and focused more on just enjoying each other's company.

From time to time, we'd see a local black duck or mallard flip about in the distance, but there was no chance of them interrupting our conversation. A pair of hen buffleheads shuttled in low from the Bay and sat among our diver decoys for nearly an hour as we continued to chat. There was no circling, no hooking into the wind for these two. In the light wind, there wasn't much for them to think about. They just settled into the decoys and seemed content to stay for a while.

We watched as these two hens fed aggressively and then simply rested among their plastic cousins. Milo watched them intently and would occasionally glance up at me. Most likely, she was wondering why we hadn't shot or when we were planning to shoot. Fred would occasionally click his safety off and on. Milo instinctively tensed as she heard the click, sensing that she'd be called into duty in the next few seconds. She cast a disgusted glance my way as the pair flew off unscathed. It looked as though this day would pass without her getting wet.

Over the afternoon, we watched a few pairs of local black ducks lift, stretch their wings and gently settle back down to a familiar place far from our little spread. Fred pulled the cream of crab soup off the stove, and we stood in relative silence savoring it. This is exactly the reason that we love duck hunting so much. It's a social event. There is food, and the food seems to take on enhanced flavor when consumed in a duck blind. Often it's grilled sandwiches, soup or fresh seared duck breast. Prepackaged goods are permitted, but most often not the norm. Finishing our soup, we allowed Milo to handle the "prewash" prior to packing the spoons, bowls and pot back in the kitchen gear bag.

With that chore complete, we continued our conversation gazing into duckless skies. The first signal of the incoming mass wasn't the sight but rather a sound resembling the passing flight of a navy jet from Pax River. The swooshing sound got increasingly louder as Fred and I panned the horizon to find the source of the disruption to our otherwise idyllic afternoon. The calm, crisp winter air was filled with this sound that we couldn't discern. Simultaneously, we found the source. Twenty-five feathered rockets found our decoys and were descending from the stratosphere at an incredibly steep angle. The sound of their wings was loud and increasing in volume. Milo's ears perked, her eyes picking up the intruders long before we found them.

Fred and I reached for our shotguns as the birds approached the decoys with no apparent sign of slowing down. At a distance of about fifty yards and closing fast, Fred made the identification. "Ringbills!!!" he shouted as we each fired our first shots in vain. Our second shots were taken as the rocketing throng strafed the water and began a vertical escape. Two from the flock fell to the water. Our third shots were taken as we arched backward at incredible angles watching as the escapees turned on the afterburners. Laughing, we both fell backward on the back side of blind with our guns empty.

We laughed heartily, both lying on our asses on the gunnel of the boat. The whole event took about seven seconds, but it's one that will be

Calm days can make for some playful behavior in birds and hunters alike. *Paul Bramble photo.*

emblazoned on our minds for a lifetime. But that's the beauty of duck hunting. It's the shared successes and failures. It's the times when words pollute the experience. It's slurping cream of crab soup staring silently at a stunning Eastern Shore marshland and tidal creeks. It's witnessing the eagerness with which a Chocolate Lab approaches each retrieve or licks clean a bowl of soup.

It's all this and more. In this instance, it was the ringbills.

THE CASTO FLOUNDER

Plans had been set with a couple of new friends who had just moved to the area. I'm sure that there was some culture shock for them transplanting themselves from Buffalo Gap, Virginia, to Chincoteague, but they seemed to be handling the transition well. I've never been to Buffalo Gap, but I'm sure that there ain't much water there. Chincoteague is surrounded by it. What they call a hill we'd call a mountain. It's certainly a foreign environment. We'd met them at a local shindig, played volleyball with them and enjoyed one another's company.

The morning dawned promising another Delmarvalous Saturday. Our plan was to spend the day on the boat sipping on a few cold beers, riding around Chincoteague and doing a little flounder fishing. Cheryl and I dropped the boat in the water at Greenbackville and eased across the Chincoteague Bay. The rising summer sun had cleared the tops of the pines of Wildcat as we brought the Angler up on plane. Gliding across the flat, oil-like surface of the salty water in the early-morning cool is a blessing of living on the Shore. We were excited to share it with our new friends.

Things were right on schedule. Robert and Chris Casto were waiting on the dock at Memorial Park as we slid up. Quickly, we loaded their gear in the boat and cast off for the day's adventure. Chris produced a jug of Bloody Marys and four cups. The twenty-year-old rod she brought, complete with the original hooks, would be the source of much conversation throughout the day. Our first stop was the gentle drop-off near Four Mouths. After a few drifts, we'd added four fat flounder to the box. The lack of wind and rising summer sun made for a steamy Saturday by midmorning. It was agreed that it was time for a boat ride. With the rods and gear properly stowed, we each received a chilly beverage and pointed the twenty-foot center console out of Chincoteague Inlet.

The ocean was what Saxis Islanders call "slick cam." The Keeper was sent south along the shores of Metompkin Island, and our guests were thrilled

Flounder remain one of the most targeted species across Delmarva. Many flatfish are caught over offshore structure. *Bobby Graves photo.*

at the number of dolphins that we came across on the twelve-mile trip. Gargatha Inlet was easily navigable, and we swung around on the western side of the southern barrier island and beached the boat. We walked along the ocean front collecting shells and other items that had washed ashore. It's a special feeling being alone on a barrier island. There's a feeling of peacefulness that invades the soul when treading the ribbon of surf that divides the vastness of the Atlantic Ocean to the east and endless intrigue of the salt marsh on the west. There, like no other place, can one find one's particular place in the universe. The vast, mercurial, unknown of the ocean at one hand in proximity to the predictable, steadiness of the marshes on the other divided only by a trail of vanishing footsteps in the sand is a stark reminder that our time here is brief. Time and tide ruled before us and will continue to do so after we're long gone. On this day, we reveled in our place.

After a few hours of beachcombing, we found our way back to the boat, laden with treasures scavenged from the sands. Waiting for all this gear to come aboard, I prepared four rods for a little more flounder fishing. The tide was just starting to ebb as the sun shone brightly in its near–two o'clock position. The anchor was washed off and placed in the anchor locker. Robert pushed us off into the slow-running current. There was no need to start the motor. I handed each a rod baited with fresh flounder belly tipped with a fat minnow. Mrs. Casto, of course, got her grandfather's old pole. Our first drift produced a single fish, but I did notice a nice deep hole right under the beach as we drifted past the *T* and toward the inlet. The old Johnson was revived, and we slowly idled three hundred yards back to the south. Quickly, the lines were redeployed as the engine again was killed. We drifted with increasing speed as the warmed seawater exited the tidal marshes. I fired up the engine and nudged the boat to the east to make certain that we'd drift through the hole that I'd spotted on the last drift. Satisfied that our baits would drag across the inside of it, the key was switched off.

Our drift took us so close to the point of the beach that our starboard side almost touched the sand. The Hummingbird bottom machine read twenty-one feet. Happy with the drift, I placed my rod in the holder and went to the transom cooler in search of cold Budweisers. With four in hand, I began passing them out when Chris's old yellow rod doubled over, evidenced by a screaming reel. The battle played on for a few minutes in the heavy current as the boat drifted out of the inlet. It was calm—there was no danger of getting caught in the wash—so we continued to harass the young angler as the fight continued. We were certain that she had hooked a bullfish or skate. The fish stayed deep and circled sporadically. She complained that the butt of the rod was hurting her stomach, so I produced a tuna belt and affixed it around her waist. She continued to battle the behemoth as we continued to drink beer, offering "encouragement" and "suggestions" on her angling skill. When it became obvious that she, after considerable time and effort, had brought the fish somewhat near the boat, I produced the gaff to handle the end game with the bullfish. The harassment by the crew continued, as did her complaining about her arms getting tired, the belt not fitting right, her beer getting hot and several other items not fit for print.

Things changed quickly as I spotted the big flounder spinning lazily in the hard ebb of Gargatha Inlet. I watched as the top hook of the twin

By whatever name you choose, channel bass, red drum, spot tails or puppy drum, catching these brutes on topwater plugs is some of the most fun a man can have while fishing. *C.L. Marshall photo.*

hook rig, a rusty O'Shaunessy 3/0, became dislodged from the flounder's jaw and reattached itself just below the topside pectoral fin. The gaff was immediately dropped as I called for the net. It seemingly took hours for her to gently bring the fish boatside where I could slide the net under it and bring it over the gunnel. There, lying in the bottom of the boat, was the biggest flounder that I'd ever seen. Chris asked, "Is that a big one?" I just stood in awe at the doormat covering the floor of the boat. It wasn't impressive; it was huge.

I tried to control my excitement as the fish was contorted to fit into the fish box. We ran back up to the original starting point of our drift and started the process once again. Trying to get the lines back out, all I could think of was the enormous size of the flounder in the cooler. We did manage somehow to pick up two fish on the subsequent drift, all during our conversation about Chris's flounder. I explained the Virginia Saltwater Fishing Tournament Citation Program to them and how she'd receive a nice plaque once it was properly weighed and measured. The minimum weight deemed worthy of a citation at that point was six pounds. This fish was well north of that mark. We decided to hold the lines and satisfy our curiosity about the weight of this fat flounder. Out the inlet and northbound, the run to Chincoteague seemed to take an eternity.

At Daisey's Dockside, the fish measured thirty-two and a half inches in length and tipped the scales at ten pounds, eight ounces. Certainly a citation, and the season's end leader as the biggest flatfish in the VSWFT's tournament. The fish was mounted and adorned a place of prominence in their home for many years. Certainly, it sparked conversation by all who had ever fished for flounder.

THE DOG PICKED ME

Adding a new puppy to any family is a chore not to be taken lightly. In a hunting family, the addition of a new retriever is a monumental moment. So it began again for us on a unremarkable Tuesday down in Onancock, Virginia. I met my next gunning partner—I just didn't know it yet.

It had been almost seven months since my last partner left us. Over that period, we'd looked at dogs from northern Delaware to southern Virginia. Any of the dozen or so dogs that we looked at would have most likely been a good gun dog, but none really seemed to have that "connection" that I was looking for. Like Rick Abolt said, "The dog picks you." There's a lot of truth in those words.

Most folks seem to think of dog ownership as a one-directional endeavor. Most thoughts are directed toward how the dog reacts to our commands, assimilates to our homes and adheres to a predetermined expectation of what a dog should be. That differs in each situation. One of the more difficult facets is the understanding that each dog is different, and their performance or demeanor can be compared to, but should not be expected to be the same as prior experiences. The special "bond" that the dog seems to immediately form with its new owner is magical and yet so different each time. That connection was made for me by Finn, our new Chocolate Lab, and I had no choice in the matter. He immediately became our dog, but it would take a week and a little luck before we understood that.

While down in Accomack County, one of my friends mentioned that there was a good bunch of puppies coming off down in Cashville by "some fella who knows a lot about dogs." Normally, that kind of recommendation is accepted graciously, then quickly sent to the recycle bin. After my last experience, I certainly wasn't looking for just any pup. I wanted one with drive, personality and the demeanor to handle the forty or so gunning trips that he'd be part of for each of the next ten or so years. Yet, for some strange reason, I found myself on the phone with "some fella who knows a lot about dogs." I'm not quite sure how, or why, that occurred, but strangely I again found myself engaged in activity typically out of character.

Wandering around on the backroads behind Onancock, looking for some stranger's mailbox and driveway, I wondered what the hell I was thinking. Relatively quickly, I made my way up a clamshell drive to a simple rancher. The garage door was open, an older pickup was hitched to a twenty-foot center console and there was that almost forgotten sound of puppies yapping in the side yard. With a huge exhale, I stepped out of the Prius to meet "some guy who knows a lot about dogs." Walking through this man's open garage, I could see that dogs were a large part of this fella's life. A well-made whelping box remained on the cement floor. Boxes of training devices of all sizes and shapes were stacked on shelving. A few fishing rods and other traditional Eastern Shore paraphernalia were scattered about. I began to feel better about this fella.

I knocked on the door, and puppies in the side yard pen yapped at the strange sound. After a few minutes with no answer, I wandered over to view the reason I'd come this far. As I stepped into the pen, they came running. It was almost a puppy stampede. One thing was for sure: they were a playful and inquisitive bunch. Falling down on one knee, I greeted the pups and instinctively began to seek out those that I thought would work for me and those that just didn't meet my eye. Lost in the moment, I didn't see or hear the property owner come through the gate behind me. Rising, I shook his hand and introductions were made. So far, so good.

After a few minutes, the conversation turned to the dogs. I asked about the mother, and he immediately asked if I'd like to come inside his home to meet the mother of this brood. A fair-sized, well-behaved female Chocolate emerged from the crate. As he began to tell me about her and her mate, my eyes wandered intermediately between the dog and the contents of this fella's abode. A pump shotgun lay on the sofa, and I couldn't help but notice the local game warden's name and number written boldly on a sheet of paper just to my right resting on the counter that I leaned on.

I inquired about the shotgun. This "fella who knows a lot about dogs" had risen early in the morning, towed his boat down to Kiptopeke and shot

Shallow water calls for shallow-draft skiffs. A good companion is always welcome. *Jim Lewis photo*.

a couple dozen pigeons for training purposes. He'd placed a call to the local warden, a man I knew personally and met professionally, to make sure that his endeavor was legal. He promised that we'd show one of the pigeons to the puppies when we went back to them. Things were looking up.

He elaborated on the mother's accomplishments and those of the sire. It was comforting to know that this participant's breeding had been carefully selected with some expectation for good hunting stock from across the southeastern part of United States. I asked of his prior experience in this field and received the surprising answer that he had no prior experience in breeding Labs. He admitted that he had previously had some success with rabbit dogs. He then escorted me into a room laden with trophies from his rabbit dog days, with one dominating a place on honor in the room. It represented his training and ownership of the national champion. Things were looking much better.

As I was satisfied with the lineage, the disposition of the mother and the breeder, he pulled a pigeon out of the freezer and again got in the pen with the pups. Several showed interest in the bird, but the way in which a male with a blue collar found it interesting, aggressively chased it after it'd been tossed and demonstrated no aversion to picking up feathers caught my eye. What closed the deal was after the third toss, the nine-week-old Hershey-colored ball of energy lumbered back toward me dragging the bird by its head. The bird was dropped about a yard from me, and with two strides and a leap he found his way into my arms, nuzzling my face like he'd been looking for me all his life. I'd been picked. I just wasn't ready to accept it yet.

After leaving, I wasn't sure what had just occurred. Having a good amount of work in front of me, I went on about my day. Arriving at home that night, my wife and I discussed the prospects of adding a retriever to our family. It was inevitable that it would happen, but we had to be ready as a family. The final decision as to when was left up to me. For the next two days, I thought about it intermittently. Three days later, my phone rang, and the number of George Waldenmaier showed on the display. He said that the blue-collared dog was surprisingly still available and asked what I wanted to do. Without much hesitation, I told him that I wanted that dog and planned on picking him up after the weekend. The words just leapt from my lips without much thought. It was an instinctive response, as much from the gut as from the head. I was back in the game.

Rather than me picking him up, George actually delivered him to us, as he and his wife had a scheduled engagement that took them right by our house. Of equal measure, I suspect he wanted to survey the dog's new home. I was busy re-spooling a TLD 15 with braid for flounder fishing when he came walking up my driveway with the dog in his arms. The dog was a little taken by the travel and his newfound surroundings. George seemed a little reluctant to let him go. It was obvious that he cared about the welfare of his pups.

Once he calmed down a little, he was allowed to run a bit on the grass. After a couple minutes, he came my way. Whether he remembered me or not I'm unsure. He bounded over toward me with the carefree bounce only a puppy can display. When I scooped him up, he immediately began to nuzzle and enjoy being held. He seemed to relax in my arms. Once again, the dog picked me.

THE GRAND FINALE

The 2018–19 waterfowl season went down in the log books as one of the worst that our group of hunters has ever endured. One might think that with such meager results that our resolve would be tested. It was. One might also think that with feathers so seldom in the dog's mouth, we'd miss an opportunity or two to try our luck. We didn't.

As the season wore on, it became evident that our old haunts would not be producing the number of birds that we'd become accustomed to over the last decade. It also became clear that those new spots that we'd planned to try wouldn't be holding many birds either. We just simply continued to grind.

As with most years, we got a good bit of weather during the last week of the season. Hopes of a new push of birds were answered by a marginal increase in the numbers of Canada geese. A little ice concentrated what few puddle ducks we had, making for decent opportunities. With only a couple days left, we hatched a plan to revisit some of our traditional hunting areas that we'd left earlier in the year due to lack of success. Each of the three upcoming hunts were classified as long shots, but closing out the year on such hallowed grounds would be fitting.

The forecast for Thursday morning was a crisp twenty-one degrees with light winds from the northwest. An overnight low of thirteen would have certainly topped the smaller ponds and still waters with a glaze of ice. The tiny guts and creeks that mallards and teal love to waste away their daylight hours in would certainly be closed for business. Our plan was to tie a big rig on the open waters of the Pocomoke River, providing a good alternative. Forty floater goose decoys and half as many mallard decoys bobbed as naturally as possible in the swiftly ebbing tide. Nine full-bodied standing goose decoys were strategically placed around the edges of the marsh, providing a very lifelike touch to our spread.

As the guns were being loaded, four fireballs of feathers rocketed across the decoys, banked hard into the light northeast breeze, bowing their wings over the goose decoys. With necks gracefully arched back and feet extended, they planned to join our little party. Six shots later, the four drake blue-wing teals were allowed to do just that. With no dog on this hunt, we allowed them to float with the tide for a few minutes while we surveyed the skyline for other potential visitors. Two mallards came from behind us at an altitude over the top of the reeds. Dropping directly into the decoys at a distance of fifteen yards, the two were dispatched on the rise. Quickly, we dropped the blind, untied the painter from the pole on the bow and pulled the graplin anchor attached to the stern cleat. The old Yamaha 25 sputtered to life, and quickly we picked up our six birds.

The next two hours passed without any more shooting, but we were witness to more birds than we'd seen thus far in the season. There was hope for the last couple days. By nine o'clock we sat in Market Street Deli feasting on scrapple, egg and cheese sandwiches with six fine birds laid neatly across the middle seat of the sixteen-foot aluminum boat. It was one of our most successful hunts of the year. Work would prevent an afternoon hunt, but plans were made to check on a small freshwater branch after work. If it

Courtesy Joyce Northam.

had remained ice free, it would certainly provide a good opportunity in the coming morning. Our check confirmed what we believed, and plans were made to give it a go in the morning.

In the darkness of a still Friday morning, we loaded the four wheelers for a short trip through the woods and fields to where the little gunning skiff lay waiting. The twelve-foot Sears Gamfisher had an eight-horsepower air-cooled engine hung on the transom with a homemade mud motor attachment. This configuration didn't make for a speedy trip, but it ensured that we would be able to safely navigate the soft, silty bottom and skinny waters that would make up most of this morning's trip. Over the second split we'd found good numbers of birds there, but with the balmy weather and lack of natural food they'd moved on. New birds were the key to success here, and the patchy ice that topped much of the headwater in this creek would aid as well.

There was no need for a big spread here. Six Avian X black duck decoys were gingerly laid in the water so as to prevent any ice from forming on the top of them. Deliberately, we set them in pairs and in a semicircle to emulate paired groups at the end of the season. It sounded like a great plan to us. We weren't sure about how the ducks would feel about it. That question was answered as we poured coffee and chatted quietly about just exactly when legal shooting time might be as four black ducks circled once and fell into the middle of the semicircle. We knew that they wouldn't be able to lie there for the full five minutes until we were able to whack them, and for fear of them

Three decoying teal turning into the wind, preparing to fall in decoys, will get the pulse racing and the dog wet. *Paul Bramble photo*.

Skirting a saltmarsh on a good flood tide is one of the true pleasures of living along the shores of the Chesapeake. *Paul Bramble photo*.

swimming off down the branch and pulling every other duck that came our way we decided to flush them off. The sound of our coffee cups clanking together in a toast to our upcoming day sent them off to another destination, hopefully a good distance from our little spread.

As legal shooting time came and went, we wondered if we had made a mistake. That question was satisfied as a single dropped in without circling. My partner planned to take him on the rise. I couldn't help but chuckle as his first shot missed a good three feet to the right of the rising bird. I chose not to shoulder my gun, but that decision looked worse by the second as his second shot failed to connect. The bird continued to rise, now nearly to the treetops, when he finally connected with his third shot. Pleasantries were exchanged as two more came from behind, banked hard to our right and made their plans known to all that they were inbound.

Just prior to calling the shot, a couple words of encouragement were sent to my partner. He responded by rolling out the trailing bird before I was able to get a good bead on the black in the lead. Losing sight of the bird as it blended with the mottled background of cypress trees and cedar in the dim morning light, I waited what seemed like an eternity for the bird to reappear to my left. Finally, I was able to make out the target and added another to our bag. This was a small miracle, as my concentration was interrupted by a single shot from the stern of the boat. My first thought was that he was firing at my bird—seeing it not fall, my attention was brought back to the matter at hand. He had added a wood duck to the mix—it had decoyed under the black duck that I was so focused on.

Finley, in his first year, quickly mopped up the downed birds. He seemed to enjoy the quick pace to which this hunt had lent itself. We'd been hunting for fifteen minutes, and he'd spend most of it in the water. The little Chocolate was coming along quite nicely.

Three blacks fell in from over the trees to the east. A single shot sent the lead bird cartwheeling across the water and up to the edge of the marsh on the far side. Finley saw it all and was off as the bird hit the water. Swimming strong with confidence and whimpering with desire along the way, he saw the wily black duck climb up on the bank with his right wing in tow. Finn hit the shoreline and pounced on the escaping duck, clamping it firmly in his jaws by the back of the neck. He knew he'd done something special and proudly brought the bird back to the boat. With that, we unloaded our guns and called it a day. We'd found a limit of blacks and a bonus wood duck and watched my new pup grow in confidence and ability.

It was a fitting way to end our season.

THE GREAT EXMORE PHEASANT HUNT

It was with pride that I pulled the new Browning A-5 Magnum out of my car in the Broadwater Academy parking lot and handed it to the school's headmaster, a man I respectfully knew only as Mr. Hanes. With several friends around, he shouldered and swung it at an imaginary passing bird, complimenting me on how it "felt" on his shoulder. We chatted a little about how the plug should be modified, how the rings should be placed, and he offered a few maintenance tips from his experience with a similar shotgun. As the bell rang, calling all students to their home room for attendance, he put the Browning back in my hands. Chuckling, he asked me if I knew what a woman and a gun had in common. I told him that I did not know that answer. I'll never forget his response: "If you learn how to hold them, they'll both treat you right." Laughing, I tossed it on the backseat and began the walk to check in with Mrs. Goffigan.

Back in the early '80s, it was commonplace for my friends and I to have a shotgun or two in the car. Most likely we'd been hunting in the morning before school or had plans to go immediately following the dismissal bell. As seniors, we weren't required to be on campus when we didn't have class. This scenario offered tremendous opportunity for hunting during midday and the early afternoon hours. Often we had to return around three o'clock for some sort of practice or similar after school event. Ducks, small game, the occasional deer and upland game were all targets for our gang of young hunters.

Our group of hunters had many options with when it came to hunting. From Miona to Kiptopeake, we had access to some of the finest hunting that the Eastern Shore of Virginia had to offer. From hunting small irrigation farm ponds for widgeon in Bayford to sitting in drainage ditches of corn stubble calling flock after flock of geese to the decoys near New Church, we had it good.

Cold temperatures had iced in most of the creeks on the Shore. The small feeder creeks were tight. The larger pieces of water featured some open water but remained mostly impassable. On two consecutive mornings, we'd noticed a small cove that opened on the first of the ebb tide and remained open until the incoming brought the ice back in the creeks. As the flowing water moved the ice bayward, large numbers of ducks funneled to the open water. It started with the puddlers, blacks at first, then mallards by the score. But it was the canvasbacks that really caught our attention. Coming up the Occohannock Creek at an altitude of about five hundred feet, the sloppy Vs were making their way toward the unencumbered cove where they could feed on the small invertebrates and assorted grasses in the shallows. We hatched a pretty good plan on how to get to them between our last class on Monday and football practice. We had the whole weekend to think about what lay in store.

The classes of that Monday morning seemed to drag on forever. Each successive period seemed to be longer than the previous. With a thirty-minute break in the morning classes, Clarry Ellis and I found our way to the Camaro. We were to pick up some chicken from Joan and Larry's and two boxes of shells from the Western Auto in Exmore. Hanging a left out of the Broadwater parking lot, our first stop would be to pick up the duck loads. As we encountered the first sharp right turn, just before Silver Beach Road, there stood in the middle of the soybean field a pair of ringneck pheasants. We couldn't believe our eyes.

Pheasants had been introduced in pockets along the Eastern Shore on several occasions, but the lack of limestone in the soil proved to be detrimental to their survival. Birds had also been introduced at Eastern Shore Outfitters down in Jamesville; these two survivors could have come from either scenario. But Clarry and I agreed that this opportunity took precedent over our other errands. With twenty-two minutes before we were due back in class, we came up with a plan that we believed was workable.

These two birds were almost in the middle of a strip of farmland that was bordered by two rather large drainage ditches. I dropped Clarry off by the ditch to the north, and he quietly began to cover the 120 yards under the cover of the ditch. I parked the car around the corner, grabbed my

Arnold Ray Evans's old scow sits tied to his dock ready to begin adventures on another day. *Jim Lewis photo.*

Browning and quickly hopped in the ditch on the south side of the birds. Neither of us had ever killed a pheasant, and the likelihood of bagging one of these two was slim.

The two or so inches of water, brambles and assorted stubble in the bottom of the ditch ensured our stalk wouldn't be a quiet one. The wind was in my favor, as it gusted to fifteen miles per hour from the north, leaving me on the downwind side. Most likely they wouldn't hear my approach, but they would certainly hear my partner making his approach. I hustled through the bottom of the ditch, not daring to look to the field until I had made nearly a hundred yards from the road. When I finally poked my head up and peered into the field, there stood the pair not more than thirty-five yards from my position. Apparently, they had become wise to Clarry's approach on the far side of the field and slowly moved downwind toward my position.

My decision was instantaneous. As I snapped up over the side of the ditch, the two flushed immediately. My first shot found nothing but air. I felt the desperation creep in as I paused to make sure that my second effort connected. At forty yards, the load of number six lead shot did its job. A cloud of feathers fell slowly earthward, reaching its destination long after the

Attentive and alert, a retriever is much more than a valuable hunting tool, a good friend. *Paul Bramble photo.*

bird fell to the bean stubble. With one remaining shot, I pulled on the hen but chose not to pull the trigger. Clarry and I met at the bird. He picked it up, and we took a minute or so to admire the fruit of our collaborative effort. He then asked if I knew who owned this field. I wasn't sure, but I thought I had a pretty good idea. I also knew that we wouldn't be welcomed if found hunting there. Clarry added that our headmaster, Mr. Hanes, retained hunting rights to this particular parcel. We turned and quickly made our way back to the warmth the car. Our pheasant was neatly placed in the trunk and our shotguns tossed on the backseat.

The shells would have to wait, but picking up the chicken we'd ordered was a must. With that done, we made it back to school before the beginning of our last class of the day. We told a few friends about our pheasant adventure. As in any high school setting, word can spread quickly. Soon, the entire student body knew of our escapade. It also made its way to Mr. Hanes. He intercepted us on our way to our afternoon duck hunt and requested our presence in his office. We tried to play it cool, but it was no use. He asked questions, and we answered honestly. We asked if he wanted to see the pheasant. He declined. It was obvious that he was not happy with our deed, but after ten minutes of admonishment, he let us roll to our afternoon encounter on the Occohannock.

We made many memories during our after-school hunting escapades, but successfully stalking Mr. Hanes's pheasant topped the bill. That bird hangs on my office wall to this day. It serves as a reminder of a good man, good friends and a good second shot.

THE MISSES

The fat drake mallard circled our boat blind twice before committing to the dozen plastic decoys bobbing somewhat lifelike on the gentle ebbing tide. The sun had broken the horizon to the east, and the first golden rays glancing off the incoming mallard's head made for a green that won't soon leave my mind. Finley sat patiently on the bow watching the events unfold to what would surely be another chance to taste feathers.

At a distance of twenty-five yards, the bird's orange feet extended as he began final decisions on where to set down. As the bird hovered over the decoys, I rose to close the deal. It was a shot I'd made hundreds of times. The bird had worked exactly how I'd hoped to the position over the decoys that would provide the easiest shot. As I shouldered the gun, the bird, as expected, found something amiss and began his escape. As I squeezed off the first shot, I expected to see the bird fall just beyond the decoys. To my shock, no feathers flew. The bird did not fall but rather caught the slight southwestern wind in his increased his wingbeats and began a hasty exit. Not connecting on the first shot threw me off my game. I was shocked, stunned and amazed that the bird didn't end up in Finley's mouth. The follow-up was just a waste. Standing there in the boat with an empty double gun, all I could do was watch the bird fly off unharmed and much the wiser.

The good shots stay with us for quite some time, but what is it about the misses that seem to stay with us forever? Why is it that in spite of all the successes we have, these misses tend to stick with us for so long? Why is it these few times when we fail to perform as expected that drive us over the

Shallow water calls for shallow-draft skiffs. A good companion is always welcome. *Jim Lewis photo*.

A good day on the Chesapeake should not be measured by the size of the rockfish or the number of birds in the bag. We should be grateful just to be able to enjoy it. *Paul Bramble photo.*

edge? As hunters, we certainly don't think that we should connect each and every time we pull the trigger. Fast-flying teal kiting over the decoys with the wind are certainly a tough shot. Tumbling tough-skinned canvasbacks skirting the outside of the rig make most hunter's highlight reels. High fives are exchanged when one is successfully pulled off, and it's talked about over beers in the lodge at hunt's end. Scotch doubles are rare and rightly hold a place of esteem in the memory. They hold a place right beside the whiffed canvasbacks, missed mallards and waved-at woodies.

Duck hunting is a sport unlike any other. It's successes and failures are defined by each participant. For some, it's about the number of birds bagged. For others, it's about being outdoors beholding the wonders of nature. Still, for others, it's about tradition. For true duck hunters, it's about all this and more. Missing is part of the game. Those who average a dozen birds out of a box of shells are said to be good shots. It's a given that we're not going to connect each time we pull the trigger. Sometimes the misses are of an unexplained variety. It's almost as if there are no pellets in the gun.

This wingshooting thing is a very instinctive endeavor. Target speed, amount of lead, path of target and distance to target must be instantly calculated for the load to intercept its target at a precise point. Factor into the equation your brain reminding you of past unsuccessful attempts and providing information to correct past poor performance. It's a highly complex endeavor. We hope that through experience and practice that we become more selective in our choice of shots and more efficient at downing our target. Our excuses for missing are as many as there are tips to improve shooting. Some of the more popular are to keep your head down on the stock. Don't look at the barrel. You rushed the shot. My feet weren't properly set. The gun didn't mount properly. You closed an eye. You left both eyes open. You looked at the target too long. There was no follow through and on and on and on.

I can remember the sunlight gleaming off the iridescent green head of a mallard as he turned to escape after both my barrels were exhausted. I clearly remember four geese low over Michaels Marsh providing an excellent opportunity at twenty-five yards. My mind still takes me back to watching the four flying away unharmed. I remember the fifty bluebills in the decoys and many more opportunities that have gone awry. Missed shots stay with us, often much longer than those we connect on. But they don't seem to deter us from continual criticism, coaching and verbal abuse of our hunting companions. It's a part of the game that is not for the thin-skinned. But no matter how good we are, how good we think we are or how good of a game we talk, it's something that happens to all of us. If thou think not, then you've not hunted long enough.

WHY?

S tanding knee deep in the brackish Pocomoke River water staring into the distance, an overwhelming sense of belonging permeated my being. Just to my left, sitting patiently in the same water, was my six-month-old Chocolate with his gaze fixed firmly on the old Remington cradled in my arms. For the first time in 258 days, I felt as though I was where I was supposed to be.

It was the pup's first real duck hunting trip. We'd trained with retrieves through decoys and with clipped pigeons in the field and spent countless hours in the yard working on basic commands and obedience. But in my opinion, nothing prepares a gun dog for gunning more than going gunning. I was prepared for it to be a messy endeavor, and that was evidenced as the decoys were being tossed from the skiff. As the first decoy took flight, I knew immediately that it was something that the dog wasn't prepared for. No sooner was the boat tied to the stob and the command given to unload than the dog took off toward the first decoy that I'd tossed. Rather than scream until the veins popped out of the side of my neck, I waited until the decoy was successfully retrieved, admonished the pup for fetching it and redeployed it with him at heel. He didn't like it, but he listened.

As it was early afternoon, we used some of the down time for training. With a shotgun blast, I sent a dummy off into the decoys. Sending him on command, he maneuvered through the six wood duck decoys, riding the tide to his dummy, snatched it up and quickly made the return trip. With the dummy delivered to hand, we took our places and began to enjoy the afternoon.

Many don't understand why we are drawn to something as different from the mainstream as waterfowl hunting. Most can't understand why we would rise hours before the sun comes up on days where we don't have to work. They can't comprehend why we enjoy being exposed to the cold, wind, rain, snow and extreme combinations of the aforementioned that render the "mainstream" at home by the fire. The fact that we routinely exit most obligatory social engagements early if the forecast is for wind and cold weather is baffling to most. But for those of us who choose to take to the marshes each year, there's nothing absurd about it. It's a way of life that for some intrinsic reason has become part of us as waterfowl hunters.

To many, the act of purposely ending the life of another animal is something very foreign. But as a hunter, it's somewhat otherworldly to become part of the food chain. As the moment of reckoning comes, it's a rush of adrenaline and endorphins that can be compared to nothing else. Predatory instinct

On a clear, crisp October morning, Milo sat patiently waiting for her turn to participate in the morning's wood duck hunt. *Parker Marshall photo.*

takes over as time slows down. Pulse and breathing must be controlled. A heightened sense of awareness takes over the consciousness. There's nothing like the teeter totter of relaxed observation of the surroundings shifting to highly focused apex predator occurring in a matter of seconds. There's no preparation for it. There's no substitute. It's just part of the "Why."

This day was different. I'd avoided the opening day festivities that usually adorn this public piece of marsh, opting instead for a steady pick of small speckled trout and rockfish. On this breezy Monday afternoon, I shared the entire expanse of marsh with only one other hunter. I thought of the odds of him being at the spot that we had selected to hunt. Arriving at the opening of the marsh, I was relieved to see it unoccupied. For Finn's first hunt, it was as suitable a place as I could think of and still have an opportunity for a shot at a wood duck. A small peninsula jutted out in the free-flowing gut. Decoys were placed on the south side of the tip, and the boat hid up a small gut on the north side. The walk to where the pallets were placed was only twenty yards. The broad pool of water would provide ample opportunity for a water retrieve.

As this was our opening day, it seemed to take on increased significance. The sense of belonging was something that I had felt before, always when in the marsh. Now I was sitting on a five-gallon bucket, and the dog had escaped his command and foraged in the rising water to my right. I watched as he seemed to enjoy sticking his snout under the water and blowing bubbles. Coming up for air, he'd gaze at me to make certain that I hadn't done anything exciting and he'd stick his head under again. Tiring from this, he regained his position at my left, knowing that something was about to happen, just not sure what that might be. Perhaps that is one of the things that draws me to the marshes as well.

Just to the south, I watched as a pair of wood ducks were startled by a mature bald eagle that soared about a hundred yards off the marsh. Redwing blackbirds zipped by the tall marsh grass in increasing numbers, some flocks containing over one hundred birds. The sound of David Mister cutting the last of the corn on the Lankford Farm was audible between wind gusts. I could hear someone on the Rice Farm running what sounded like a John Deere Gator, most likely resupplying his bait piles for the coming split of deer muzzleloader season. This idyllic trance was interrupted as the other hunter in the marsh cut loose a single volley. It seemed to add to the setting. I was where I should be.

With forty minutes left before the gunning day was scheduled to end, the local wood ducks began to stretch their wings before bedding down for the night. Looking to the south, a flock of nine rose from the marsh. Within

There's nothing quite like feeling that "tell-tale tap" on the bait and firmly setting the hook on a solid fish. Especially in that golden hour where the sun sits just above the bay's horizon. *Jim Emche photo.*

seconds, it was obvious that they would provide me an opportunity. Watching them dancing in the wind, instincts from long ago took over. The drake on the far right slipped out of range. The far left was marginal. The third one from the left set his wings for a second, making him my choice. With instinct honed from over fifty years of playing this game, the gun found my shoulder. The amount of lead wasn't calculated, it was known. As the shot rocked the feathered rocket, his head immediately fell back and the bird dish-ragged in to the water just to my right. There was no second shot.

Finn, the green dog on his first hunt, would be put to the test. More accurately, the time we spent together working up to this moment would be tested. My ability to communicate acceptable behavior and manipulate the pup's natural instinct hopefully would come to fruition in the next few seconds. The answer was instantaneous. There was no need for a command to send him. He saw the whole thing play out. He saw the coming birds, saw and heard the shot and saw the bird fall into the water. As the gun came off my shoulder, the dog was still at my side, staring up at me and whining. As we made eye contact, he took off across the marsh, found deeper water and swam strongly to the floating wood duck. Upon approaching the downed

Cold bluebird mornings provide great sunrises but often yield few birds in the bag. *Paul Bramble photo.*

bird, he "pounced" on it and quickly turned for the return trip. Within seconds, he was back with the bird, delivering it to hand and wanting to do it again. I made a big deal over his success, but to him it seemed to be another training exercise. I felt as though it was so much more.

For nearly fifty years, I've had folks ask me why we worked so hard and spent so much time chasing ducks. We each have our own reasons. For nearly fifty years, I've provided the same answer: it's part of who I am. It's the countless friends I've made. It's the sharing of a porkchop breakfast after a morning's hunt with old friends. It's the late nights prepping for an early-morning trip. It's the new places we get to see. It's the same old places where we find peace. It's the dogs, the guns, the successes and the failures. It's the quiet times spent with friends where no words are needed. It's the Sunday duck and dumpling dinners and so much more.

It's part of my family heritage and it's part of what makes me, and many like me, an Eastern Shoreman. As I've said before, I've tried to quit it, but it keeps calling me back. There's no denying it; there's no running from it. It baffles me why more don't experience it. I think they should.

THINGS CHANGE QUICKLY

Things in this life can change quickly. This day was no exception. The morning began as many before it. The alarm broke the bedroom silence, and Milo instantly woke from her snoring slumber and was immediately ready to roll. She knew what was coming. She had seen me packing the boat the night prior and knew from experience that that boat would not be sailing without her nose in it. As for myself, it took a bit longer to get moving.

An early-morning meeting with longtime gunning partner Anthony Thomas and a cup of hot Goose Creek coffee made the ride to Hammocks much more enjoyable. We chatted about the recent status of local hunting and prognosticated about the expectations for the morning. He and I both had obligations on this cold, windy Sunday morning. A quick duck hunt, however, wouldn't interfere with either of our schedules.

On the commute, Milo sometimes sat patiently. When the anticipation of the coming hunt became too much for her Labrador heart to bear, she quickly paced the width of the truck several times before once again settling in directly behind me with her muzzle on my shoulder. She was as excited as we were.

At the ramp, we were alone again. The tide was half high and falling. We were to have little trouble navigating the muddy shallow waters of Messongas Creek up to our favorite spot, dubbed the Spankbox.

The boat was easily launched as Milo performed her usual morning ritual in the thin strip of grass that borders the parking lot and riprap. Prior to

Each fall, the Delmarva Discovery Center hosts an event called Heritage Days. The event boasts one of the best collections of wildfowl artists in the region. Milo and I were happy to participate. *Mike Galeone photo.*

pulling the truck out of the ramp, per usual, Milo again found her spot on the backseat. With the truck parked, I slid on my knee boots and Sitka outer coat. As the zipper approached my chin, Milo exited the truck quickly and sprinted to the boat. Upon my arrival, she was sitting on the backseat ready to go. Though Anthony and I were excited for the morning's endeavors, our enthusiasm in no way matched that of the little Chocolate Lab.

With a few pulls of the cord, the old Yamaha 25 two stroke sputtered to life. Quickly turning the boat around to face the deeper waters of the creek, we slowly made way to the channel. With Anthony steady on the center seat, I brought the boat up on plane. Milo leaned forward as the boat accelerated. Her ears began to flap haphazardly in the breeze, and she seemed to smile. She was in her element.

The trip up the creek was uneventful. The sun wouldn't make an appearance for another forty minutes when we arrived at our blind. A dozen teal decoys were hurriedly tossed in no real arrangement near the center of the creek. A pair of black ducks were positioned inside and downwind of the teal. With that, the boat was tucked under the tall reeds on the shoreline, blocking the stiffening northwestern wind. It was actually quite comfortable with the blind pulled up. As the boat approached the shore, Milo quickly exited and took her place among the reeds. She found it easier to hunt under natural cover.

We popped up our blind and got our guns loaded two minutes past legal shooting time. As Anthony's receiver slammed shut on his Beretta, I picked off the first teal of the day. Milo was immediately in the water, picked up the bird and was on the return trip as a flock of four faced the wind just above the decoys. Three of the four fell dead. Milo delivered the first bird to hand and quickly turned to look for the results of our recent shooting. As she cruised back toward the decoys, one of the downed bird's wing flapped. Her head lowered as she struck another gear and picked up her swimming pace significantly. Firmly snatching up the wing-flopping teal, she turned to eye the other two that were down. I could see a fleeting thought of grabbing two at a time, but she thought better of it and delivered the second of the day to hand. She very efficiently handled the retrieve of the other two.

Anthony and I spent the next twenty minutes picking at a steady flight of blue- and green-wing teal. One hen bufflehead was the result of collateral damage. Milo handled her chores respectably. We needed two to cover our twelve-bird limit as a flock of three came from left to right. Our first two shots claimed our eleventh and twelfth birds of the day. Anthony's fell within ten yards of the boat. Milo scooped up that one first and delivered it to the back of the boat where my outstretched hand waited. She turned, much like an Olympic swimmer, and stroked back toward the second bird. Putting the retrieved bird in the pile, I began to unload my gun and stow my gear for the trip home. Anthony did the same as we expected the final retrieve to go as those before it. Looking up to check Milo's progress, it became obvious that neither Milo nor I could see the bird. We surmised that it had swum toward the other bank and taken shelter there in hopes

Courtesy Joyce Northam.

of escaping Milo's grasp. I sent her to the far shore. After five or so minutes of searching, she sat, awaiting further command. Finished hunting for the day, we fired up the motor and putted toward her spot on the far bank. As our bow hit the marshy bank, the drake green-wing made a break for it. Milo leapt off the bank and quickly thwarted the bird's escape, returned to the shore and jumped into the boat with the bird firmly in her muzzle. It was fitting for her last retrieve.

On the trip back to the ramp, Milo enjoyed the wind in her nose. She loved and lived for days like this. The boat was trailered, and in a matter of minutes Anthony, Milo and I were back at the shop pouring hot coffee and rehashing the events of the day. The porkchops simmered in the cast-iron skillet on the range. After breakfast, I ran Anthony back to this truck and went back to Pocomoke to exchange the sixteen-foot gunning skiff for the twenty-foot Carolina Skiff. I needed to stick some cedars around a blind down on the backside of Saxis. They were already cut and loaded in the boat. The exchange was made quickly, and Milo didn't get out of the truck. She was making sure that she wouldn't be left out of the afternoon's adventures. With the boat hooked up, we pulled out of Pocomoke thinking about all the things that I had to do over the remainder of the day and the next few days. Milo slept on the backseat during the return trip to Sanford.

Sometimes the best trips are made with just you and the dog. *Jim Lewis photo*.

With the tide now well on the rise and the northwestern wind increasing, I decided to launch at Saxis rather than Hammocks. I could run Back Creek and then hug the Tunnell's Island shoreline, staying out of the increasing wind most of the trip. I planned a short, easy trip.

The boat was easily launched, and Milo jumped aboard as I pulled the truck out of the ramp and parked it fifty yards away. It was Sunday about 2:30 p.m. She sat perched atop the cedars watching me put my boots on and begin to secure my outercoat. I pulled her bumper from the floor and began to walk back toward the boat. Milo, seeing the bumper, leapt from the boat and sprinted toward me. The right front tire of one of my lifelong friend's trucks stopped her from reaching me. At a speed of less than ten miles per hour, he had unavoidably struck my dog. With a sharp yelp, she rolled and stood wobbily on her feet as I ran to her, fearing the worst. I surveyed her situation. No bones were visibly broken. She was bleeding a bit from her mouth and in obvious pain. The driver and I both were in shock, he being very, very upset over what had occurred.

Nesting boxes require a little work in the off season. Wood ducks and a variety of puddle ducks take full advantage of them. *Paul Bramble photo.*

Milo began to try to get her senses about her as I was trying to explain to my friend that it wasn't his fault. He knew the dog and what a hunter she was. He also knew that I thought more of that dog than I did many people. He was devastated. Milo, during our discussion, ambled over to the boat and jumped in, emitting a loud squeal as her feet hit the floor of the boat. In spite of her injuries, she still had the desire to go one more time. For a moment, I thought she might be OK as I held her in the floor of that boat. But it was clear to see that her desire was no match for the injuries that she had sustained.

We lifted her out of the boat and laid her on the back seat of the truck. The trailer was unhooked. The boat was left in the ramp. She died in my arms along Route 13 en route to the vet. It is my hope that she was welcomed into heaven by Gunner and Butler, my other two gunning dogs.

The odds of this event occurring are astronomical. Fewer than five cars a day frequent this ramp on a winter's Sunday afternoon. The chances of a truck moving at ten miles per hour causing such an injury to a well-conditioned hunting machine are very slim. The whats and what ifs that surround such events will drive all parties involved crazy. It happened. There is no blame. Her ashes are now located in the location of her last hunt.

It's been said that dogs are part of our lives, but we are all of theirs. It's a situation that dog owners know they will experience at some point when they drive the pup home from the kennel. But the real thing to observe is the quickness with which permanent change can occur. There's a void now around the house that can't be replaced. At some point, the void will be filled by another hunting dog, but not replaced. But it could have just as likely been a friend, family member or stranger. Take the time to make sure you're right with those who matter. Tomorrow is promised to no one.

THREE MALLARDS TO GO

Riding along in the predawn darkness, Bruce Ennis's Ford F-350 seemed to find every pothole in the old dirt road. Precariously perched on the tailgate, my enthusiasm for this morning's hunt wasn't tempered by the rough ride or the rain pelting on the hood of my parka. We'd put in the work over six long months, and this morning's hunt was to be the last of the season. Bobby Graves, seated beside me on the tailgate, was grinning like a possum that just successfully crossed the highway. I hunkered down and held on for the ride.

Those uneducated in what it takes to be successful in duck hunting would certainly think we'd lost our minds. We thought we had all the bases covered. Brush had been cleared, blinds built and bushed, water levels dropped, grain planted, grain fertilized, water levels adjusted to proper level to support puddle ducks and many more details tended to. The late-winter freeze had shut down most water hunts, and we'd been bouncing from field to field finding excellent opportunity with both geese and mallards. Our pond had held some birds prior to the freeze. Desperate to hold on to them, we rigged an ice eater to a gasoline-powered generator in an effort to keep part of our pond open.

Upon arrival to our blind, Bobby and I slid off the tailgate. Bruce bounded out of the cab, and the three of us were pleased to find a forty-yard swatch of open water in front of our box. Quickly, the mallard and black duck decoys were deployed along with four standing field goose decoys on the sandy stretch to the left of the box. Nestling into the box with the tall pines

Mallards are one of the more popular targets for waterfowlers anywhere. It's for good reason; they're delicious! *Paul Bramble photo.*

to our backs, we were sheltered from the stiff northwestern winds. Actually, it was quite cozy. I set the phone alarm to legal shooting time as we loaded our guns in preparation for what we hoped would come. We sat in silence sipping coffee and nibbling on fresh Dunkin' Donuts, watching and listening to the morning come alive.

The predawn was alive with waterfowl of all types vying for position in our little slice of open water. We marveled at the sound of woodies wings slapping against the small twigs as they twisted and turned to prevent from slamming into tree trunks. Mallards cautiously circled before finding the area an acceptable place to visit. The blacks just threw caution to the wind and piled right in. After what seemed like an eternity, the phone vibrated, and we began to devise a plan for the birds that swam nervously on the open water. The overcast sky occluded the coming sun. Slight Vs could be seen cutting across the pond's surface, but it was still too dark to make out a ducklike form to fashion a good, clean shot. Ducks continued to pour in.

For another ten minutes, we watched and waited. Now standing in the blind with guns in hand, we spoke in hushed voices about what we could see or thought we could see. Four wood ducks dropped over the trees behind us into the pond just twenty yards away. Seeing them land. we had a good visual on them. The shot was called as the four, along with the other twenty ducks swimming around the pond, took flight. Our first four shots claimed three of the four woodies. Bruce and I were looking to the left of the blind as two speedsters banked hard from the left and got past us as we were reloading. Bobby's Beretta belched fire twice, sending both tumbling across the surface of the water. There was that grin again.

Six or so came and went, interrupting our good-natured ribbing of Graves. A single sailed in from the right, and Bruce deposited him directly in front of the blind. Several of the six we had down floated with their white breast up, flaring several incoming flocks of birds. We decided to pick up our downed birds. Bruce jumped in the canoe and paddled quickly to the four floating in front of the blind. I eased down the bank and picked up one. The last bird that Bruce shot had made its way to the base of the blind and lay motionless in the stuck pines. Walking back to the box, I helped Bruce pull the canoe ashore, grabbed the birds and hastily made my way back to the box. Bruce, donning waders, walked in front of the blind to pick up the remaining downed bird. He seemed to take his time doing it. The bird was positioned beautifully on the pine straw, such that he decided to snap a few pictures of it with his phone. After several pics were taken. the phone was stashed in his waders' waterproof pouch. As he then reached for the drake wood duck, the bird scurried around his outstretched hand and immediately took flight. He watched in awe as our "Lazarus" bird came back to life and flew to the safety of the woods. Bruce just stood there and watched. It was all he could do.

I had walked twenty or so yards to the right of blind, looking for any other birds that we may have knocked down. Seeing none, I had begun my trek back to the box. As the bird made his escape from Bruce, his path would provide me with a redemption shot. With only one shot left in my Remington 20, I was looking forward to the bragging rights that this bird would provide over the coming months. With a little smile on my face, I shouldered the gun, applied the appropriate lead and squeezed off my only remaining round. The bird continued its trajectory and disappeared over the far tree line unscathed.

Action slowed somewhat over the next few minutes. A single woody fell over the trees in front of the blind and maintained a low and direct flight toward our decoys. At twenty yards, I shouldered the Remington 20 gauge and squeezed off a single shot as the bird's wings bowed. It fell neatly just outside of the decoys. Just as the last of the feathers hit the water, five settled outside the decoys. Bruce and Bobby each claimed one on the rise.

A healthy greenhead rising from the decoys provides a sporting opportunity. *Paul Bramble photo.*

The wind had increased significantly with the rising sun. Rain continued to steadily beat the surface of our little pond. Our nine wood ducks had made for an excellent morning. Pouring another cup of coffee, we began to recap our good fortune of the morning. It was a fitting conclusion to a good season. Sitting in the box, sheltered from the wind, rain and real world, we reminisced about the ups and downs of the season. Plans were made for improving our lot in the upcoming year. As discussion began to turn to packing it in for the day, the gentle quacking of a hen mallard interrupted our discussion. Rolling out a few notes on the Eastern Shoreman Timber call, we saw the three mallards circle once, twice and then commit to the decoys. Two drakes and a hen began their descent and hung just over the decoys abreast of one another. It was the perfect shot to end our day. In unison, three shots rang out. In unison, the three mallards fell to the calm waters of our secluded pond. Our day was over.

After the birds were retrieved, the decoys and canoe was tossed in the truck. The ride back down that same old bumpy dirt road didn't seem so bad as riding out, especially after the show those three mallards gave us. It was the perfect ending to an outstanding hunt.

TIDE RUNNERS

In the early 1980s, gray trout fishing was the norm. There seemed to be an unlimited supply of two-to-five-pounders scattered throughout the Pocomoke and Tangier Sounds. They were plentiful and pulled many a "retired" fisherman off the sofa in hopes of turning a tiderunner into a fresh fish sandwich.

They could be found in late May on the grassy flats now inhabited by vast numbers of rays and striped bass. Shallow water rocks held smaller fish; deeper haunts, such as Robin Hood, Byrds Rock and California Rock, held larger fish. The Target Ships, located on the west side of Tangier Island, were arguably the best place to consistently find nine-pound-plus citation-winning fish.

These two pre-*Dreadnought* battlewagons, the *Alabama* and the *Indiana*, were among a total of seven ships that were subjected to test firing by the navy beginning as far back as 1911. Once towering twenty feet above the waterline, remnants of these two steel-hulled, coal-fired war veterans have been bombed and shot into submission over the years. Another, the *San Marco*, was bombed with such ferocity that only a small profile of it exists today under twenty feet of water. The other two provide haven for smaller finfish, crabs and other morsels that larger species, such as jumbo gray trout, find delicious.

The maze of twisted metal above the water gave only a small glimpse into the mess that lies hidden by the waters of the Chesapeake. This maze was a tackle-eating monster. Top and bottom rigs had no chance of survival.

Having the opportunity to harvest such a delectable food source as speckled trout is a perk of living near the Chesapeake. *Paul Bramble photo.*

Fish-finder rigs were rendered useless. The most consistent way to entice the fish from the depths, and get them in the boat, was through using a three-quarter to one-ounce bucktail, adorned with a purple firetail worm. Old-school anglers added a small chunk of peeler for good measure. These contraptions were lobbed toward the structure and gingerly bounced off the bottom structure. Many were lost, some on the first cast. But that was the price to pay for the opportunities that swarmed around the sunken ships.

Though the Chesapeake and these Target Ships off Tangier were among the best places to fish, no place held the allure of the Delaware Bay. Brown Shoal and Fourteen Foot Light teemed with large fish, many topping the ten-pound mark with regularity. The world record came from there, and that is precisely where Paige Linton and I were headed on a calm, sunny, Thursday afternoon. The local papers and fish rags populated their pages weekly with grinning anglers posing with their prizes. It'd been a good season thus far, but those massive trout were the things dreams are made of. We wanted in.

Meeting in Laurel, Delaware, Paige and I towed his twenty-one-foot Parker toward Lewes. Loaded and launched, we pulled up the Loran numbers, plugged in the waypoint and let the Raynav 580 point the way to Brown Shoal. By Chesapeake Bay standards, it was a short run. Tying on white one-ounce bucktails on the way out, I soaked in the new surroundings. I could see the ferry's stern as it chugged toward Cape May. The expansive riprap and ice breaks all looked like places that fish would congregate. Our sights were set on where we'd heard the fish were being caught.

In short order, we came off plane and idled among a pack of twenty-five or so fellow fishermen. It was obvious that we'd come to the right spot. Rods were bent, nets dipped silver-bellied trophies and the sounds of fishermen's successes and failures filled the summer air. As Paige worked to position our boat to find an unencumbered drift, I tried to focus on cutting the peelers for bait. With all the commotion going on around us, it was a little hard to concentrate. When the Yamaha 150 was slid into neutral, I handed Paige his baited rod and set mine into freespool. The sinking bucktail found the bottom in a few seconds. With a couple cranks, I had achieved a good, taut line providing sensation, or "feel," as the bucktail slid across the sandy bottom. Lifting the rod tip, I brought the jig up about a foot off the bottom. Its freefall was interrupted by a telltale tap. Setting the hook on weakfish is a tenuous event. Too harsh a hook set will rip the hook free from their tender mouths. Too little, and they will escape with the bait, not finding the barb. The soft tip of the Diawa Sealine rod was an asset. Lifting the rod in

Small jigs slowly fished above a grass bed tricked this trout for angler Jay Fleming. *Paul Bramble photo.*

a smooth transition to a position resembling ten o'clock, the line came taut. The first run pulled a steady stream of pink Ande monofilament off the Abu-Garcia 5500.

Within a few minutes, the gentle game of tug of war ended as Paige slid the net under the largest gray trout that I'd ever seen. This fish was as long as my leg and sported a very impressive girth. After admiring the fish for a minute or so, it was deposited in the ice and the bucktail reloaded with a new worm and hunk of peeler. Though no scientific data can back up this claim, it is my opinion that there is no better bait for trout (gray or spotted seatrout) than the ripe shell of a peeler just before it molts. Paige hooked up his first of the day as I was preparing to send my bait down for another try. His solid ten-pounder was netted and laid beside my fish in the cooler. My second drop confirmed my belief in my bait of choice.

We continued to catch fish consistently for nearly three hours. Seven fish were kept, and certainly over twenty were released. The tide slowed and so with it the bite. Heading back to the dock, we rehashed the events of the evening and gawked at the size of the fish. If those we were catching at the target ships were extra large, then these were whalers. With the boat loaded and safely delivered back to Paige's residence, I loaded my gear in the red

Early-fall light tackle jigging for rockfish is a favorite activity for outdoorsmen all across the Chesapeake Region. *Rick Huey photo.*

Ford Bronco and headed for home. On the way home, I tried to guess how much the larger fish weighed. It was certainly over ten pounds but by how much I really couldn't fathom. The fish remained on ice over night.

After a good night's sleep, I unloaded my fishing gear and left the fish-filled cooler in the truck and headed for Bozo Godwin's crab shanty down in Sanford. Bozo's was an official weigh station for the Virginia Saltwater Tournament and for that had a set of certified scales. I told Bozo that I had a caught a few trout and would like to see how much they weighed. When I produced the first, and largest, from the cooler his first question was predictable. "Where'd you catch that hog? The Target Ships?" he immediately quipped. Dodging the question, I asked what he thought it'd weigh. He guessed twelve. It tipped the scales at fourteen pounds, four ounces. The question of where it was caught surfaced several more times. I told him that I'd fished with someone else who swore me to secrecy. He continued to press. I declined to fill out the citation form, which should have been a giveaway that it wasn't caught in Virginia. Finally, he guessed that I'd caught the fish at Robin Hood. I remained silent on the subject.

Those seven fish weighed seventy-seven pounds.

The boats were thick as I'd ever seen for the next ten or so days at Robin Hood.

ABOUT THE AUTHOR

C.L. Marshall is a lifelong Eastern Shoreman and longtime journalist. He's a former editor of *Shore Golf* magazine and the *Fisherman* magazine. His previous books include *Chesapeake Bay Duck Hunting Tales* and *Hunting and Fishing the Chesapeake*, as well as two cookbooks, *A Taste of Eastern Shore Living* and *A Taste of Delmarva Living*. To find out more about Marshall and his upcoming events, check out his website at www.chesapeakebaybooks.net.

MAY 2 7 2021